ALL ABOUT THE *Dollar*

...makes me want to holler...

JEROME ALBAN KIRKLAND SR.

outskirts press

Outskirts Press, Inc.
http://www.outskirtspress.com

ISBN: 978-1-9772-2859-8

Outskirts Press and the "OP" logo are trademarks belonging to Outskirts Press, Inc.

PRINTED IN THE UNITED STATES OF AMERICA

All About the Dollar:
"It makes me want to holler,
makes me want to scream,
it's not about the color white,
not about the color black,
but all about the color green!"

Dedication

This book is dedicated to my family, close friends, and community of individuals who lack financial literacy and financial discipline. If you would like to help change the current situation regarding financial literacy among the poorest Americans, you can support the GoFundMe campaign sponsored by Kirkland Financial Group to provide financial counseling to those who can least afford it.

This book is dedicated to the 38.1 million Americans currently living in poverty (according to the 2018 Census Bureau Report). Within this group lies roughly 25 million senior Americans of age 60 or older who are living below 250% of the federal poverty level. These are Americans who were unable to prepare for the "golden days." When you get to your senior years "the struggle is real." Don't become a statistic in your last days. Start planning now regardless of your age.

I would like to take this opportunity to make special mention of Ms. Jenise E. Ramos, my closest friend and ally during a time in my life when the chips were down. She never accepted less from me than what she knew I could deliver. As a diabetic from a very young age, she never made excuses, working two jobs at times to care for herself and her daughter. I call her an "old soul" who has been here before because she is so wise and knows how to make a dollar "holler!" I especially dedicate the chapter on "The Struggle is Real" to her because she taught me the true meaning. She was and always will be my rock, joy, and source of daily inspiration. I will always love her with all my heart even though she was only in my life for a season. She will always remain a lifetime friend. No time, distance, or circumstance will ever separate us.

I also dedicate this book to my two lifelong friends whom I have known for more than 40 years. Our relationships have stood the test of time through every trial and tribulation. These two friends are Mr. Patrick B. Lee and Ms. Donna D. Williams.

Lastly, I dedicate this book to my three children, Jerome Jr, Aaron Sr and Janice. In addition, I leave this book as a legacy and testament to my three grandchildren, Aniyah, Aaron Jr and Sabrina. I hope this book serves as a blueprint for helping them to get off to a healthy financial lifestyle at a very young age.

The title of this book is derived from a slogan that I used to promote my financial radio broadcast show over a decade ago. The slogan goes like this: "It's all about the dollar, makes me want to holler, makes me want to scream, it's not about the color white, nor about the black, it's all about the color green!"

Author Jerome Kirkland

Table of Contents

CHAPTER 1

What is money?

Definition: Money is defined as 1. Any circulating medium of exchange including coins, paper money, and demand deposits. 2. Any article or substance used as a medium of exchange.

Everyone uses money. We all want it, work for it, and think about it. While the creation and growth of money seems somewhat intangible, money is the way we get the things we need and desire. The task of defining what money is, where it comes from, and what it's worth belongs to those who dedicate themselves to the discipline of economics.

The History of Money

Before the development of a medium of exchange people would barter to obtain goods and services they needed. Two individuals, each possessing some goods the other wanted, would enter an agreement to trade.

However, this early form of barter does not provide the transferability and divisibility that makes trading efficient. For instance, if you have cows but need bananas, you must find someone who not only has bananas but also the desire for meat. What if you find someone who has the need for meat but no bananas and can only offer you bunnies? To get your meat, he or she must find someone who has bananas and wants bunnies…and so on.

The lack of transferability of bartering is tiring, confusing, and inefficient, but that is not where the problems end. Even if you find someone with whom to trade meat for bananas, you may not think a bunch of them is worth a whole cow. You would then have to devise a way to divide your cow (a messy business) and determine how many bananas you are willing to take for certain parts of your cow.

To solve these problems came *commodity money*, a type of good that functions as currency. In the 17th and early 18th centuries, for example, American colonialists used beaver pelts and dried corn in transactions. Assigned generally accepted values, these commodities were used to buy and sell other things. The kinds of commodities used for trade were widely desired, and therefore valuable, but they were also durable, portable, and easily storable.

Another more advanced example of commodity money is a precious metal like gold, which for centuries was used to back paper currency until the 1970s. In the case of the American dollar, for example, this meant that foreign governments were able to take their dollars and exchange them at a specified rate for gold with the US Federal Reserve. What's interesting is that, unlike the beaver pelts and dried corn (which can be used for clothing and food, respectively), gold is not necessarily useful. After all, you can't eat it, and it won't keep you warm at night; but the majority of people think it is beautiful and they know others think it is beautiful, so gold is something you can safely believe has worth. Gold, therefore, serves as a physical token of wealth based on people's perception.

If we think about this relationship between money and gold, we can gain some insight into how money gains its value – as a representation of something valuable.

The second type of money is *fiat* money, which does away with the need for a physical commodity to back it. Instead, its value is set by supply and demand, and people's faith in its worth. Fiat money developed because gold was a scarce resource and quickly growing economies couldn't always mine enough to back their currency supply requirements. For a booming economy, the need for gold to give money value is extremely inefficient, especially when its value is really created through people's perception.

Fiat money becomes the token of people's perception of worth, the basis of a currency's value. A growing economy is doing a good job of producing goods that are valuable to itself and to other economies. Generally, the stronger the economy, the stronger its money will be perceived and sought after, and vice versa. But remember, this perception, although abstract, must somehow be backed by how well the economy can produce specific goods and services that people want.

Full Faith and Credit and the Value of Money

In 1971 the US dollar was taken off the gold standard. The dollar was no longer redeemable in gold, and the price of gold was no longer fixed to any dollar amount. This meant that it was now possible to create more money than there was gold to back it. It is the health of the American economy that backs the dollar value. If the economy takes a nosedive, the value of the US dollar will drop both domestically through inflation, and internationally through currency exchange rates. Fortunately, the implosion of the US economy would plunge the world into a financial dark age, so many other countries and entities are working tirelessly to ensure that never happens.

Nowadays, the value of money (not just the dollar, but most currencies) is decided purely by its purchasing power as dictated by inflation. That is why simply printing money will not create wealth for a country. Money is created by a kind of a perpetual interaction between concrete things, our palpable desire for them, and our abstract faith in what has value. Money is valuable because we want it, but we want it only because it can get us a desired product or service.

This is what we refer to as *full faith and credit.*

What is full faith and credit and what does it meant to potential investors? Full faith and credit is a phrase used to describe the unconditional guarantee or commitment offered to an entity to back the interest and principal of another entity's debt. The full faith and credit commitment is typically employed by a government to help lower borrowing costs of a smaller, less stable government or a government-sponsored agency. This can be adopted on a global level between countries or within a country like the US.

In the US, the Treasury Department issues bills, notes, and bonds as a means of borrowing money from the public to fund the government's capital projects.

These securities require that interest payments be made to lenders and investors periodically. On the maturity date, bondholders expect full payment of the face value of the securities. To encourage investors to purchase the debts issues, the treasuries are backed by the full faith and credit of the government, providing assurance to fixed income investors that the expected interest payments and principal repayments will be made regardless of the economic situation.

Because Treasury securities are backed by the full faith and credit of the government, they are referred to as "risk free securities." The government cannot default on its obligations as it has the power to print more money or increase taxes in order to repay its debt. In addition, the interest rate on these risk-free securities also acts as the benchmark rate for other fixed income securities that have some level of risk. In effect, the interest rate applied to debt instruments with risk is the risk-free rate plus a premium determined by the riskiness of the bond.

Risk-averse investors looking for safe investments typically go for securities that are backed by the full faith and credit of the government. These securities offer lower yields than securities with more risk. However, investors are willing to accept the low yield in return for preserving their investment and expected interest income.

Debt issued by a smaller government entity, such as a municipality, may also be backed by the full faith and credit of the issuer. General obligation municipal bonds are payable from the municipality's general funds and are backed by the full faith and credit of the municipal issuer which may have unlimited authority to tax residents to pay bondholders.

On rare occasions, the federal government may step in to back a portion of the payment obligations of municipalities by its full faith and credit. For example, during the "credit crisis" of 2009, investors shied away from municipal bonds. To encourage lenders to invest in these securities the US Treasury subsidized 35% of interest payments to investors and municipal issuers through a bond program known as Build America Bonds.

The Government National Mortgage Association (Ginnie Mae) is one example of a government agency that is backed by the full faith and credit of the US government. Securities backed by Ginnie Mae mortgages have lower yields than other mortgage-backed securities (MBS) because they are assumed to carry less risk due to the federal government's backing.

How Much Money is Out There, Really?

Now that we know what money is and what gives it value, exactly how much money is out there and what forms does it take? Economists and investors ask this question every day to see whether there is inflation or deflation. To make money more discernible for measurement purposes, they have separated it into categories.

M1 – This category of money includes all physical denominations of coin and currency, demand deposits, which are checking accounts and NOW accounts, and traveler's checks. This category of money is the narrowest of the three; it's essentially the money used to buy things and make payments.

M2 – With broader criteria this category adds all the money found in M1 to all short-term deposits, saving accounts deposits, and non-institutional money market funds. This category represents money that can be readily transferred into cash.

M3 – The broadest class of money, M3 combines all money found in the M2 definition and adds to it all longer-term time deposits, institutional money market funds, short term repurchase agreements, and other larger liquid assets.

By adding these three categories together, we arrive at a country's money supply, or the total amount of money within an economy.

The M1 category includes what's known as active money – that is, the total value of coins and paper currency in circulation among the public. The amount of active money fluctuates seasonally, monthly, weekly, and daily. In the United States, Federal Reserve Banks distribute new currency for the US Treasury Department. Banks lend money out to customers, which becomes classified as active money once it is circulated.

The variable demand for cash equates to a constantly fluctuating active money total. For instance, people typically cash paychecks or withdraw from ATM's over the weekend, so there is more active cash on a Monday than a Friday. Another example is the decline in public demand for cash following the December holiday season.

Now that we've discussed why and how money is created in the economy, we need to touch on how a country's central bank (for the US, that would be the Federal Reserve Bank) can influence and manipulate its money supply.

Let's look at a simplified example of how this is done. If the central bank wants to increase the amount of money in circulation, it can simply print it, but the physical bills are only a small part of the money supply.

Another way for the central bank to increase the money supply is to buy government fixed-income securities on the market. When the central bank buys these government securities, it puts money into the marketplace and effectively into the hands of the public. How does a central bank such as the Federal Reserve pay for this? As strange as it sounds, they simply create money out of thin air and transfer it to those people selling the securities.

Central banks can also lower interest rates, allowing banks to extend low cost loans or credit – a phenomenon known as cheap money – and encouraging businesses and individuals to borrow and spend.

To shrink the money supply, the central bank does the opposite and sells government securities. The money with which the buyers pay the central bank is essentially taken out of circulation. Keep in mind that we are generalizing in this example to keep things simple.

Remember, as long as people have faith in the currency, a central bank can issue more of it. But if the Fed issues too much money, the value will go down, as with anything that has a higher supply than demand. So, even though technically it can create money "out of thin air," the central bank cannot simply print money as it wants.

Manipulating the Money Supply

In the 17th century, Great Britain was determined to keep control of the American colonies and the natural resources they supplied. To do this, the British limited the money supply and made it illegal for the colonies to mint coins of their own. Instead, the colonies were forced to trade using English bills of exchange that could only be redeemed for English goods. Colonists were paid for their goods with these same bills, effectively cutting them off from trading with other countries.

In response, the colonies regressed back into a barter system using ammunition, tobacco, nails, pelts, and anything else that could be traded. Colonists also gathered whatever foreign currencies they could, the most popular being the large silver Spanish dollars. These were called "pieces of eight" because when you had to make change, you pulled out your knife and hacked it into eight bits. From this, we have the expression "two bits," meaning a quarter of a dollar.

Massachusetts was the first colony to defy the mother country. In 1652, the state minted its own silver coins, including the Oak Tree and Pine Tree Shillings. It circumvented the British law stating that only the monarch of the British empire could issue coins by taking advantage of the fact that between 1649 and 1660, England was a republic and during this period there was no monarch. In 1690, Massachusetts issued the first paper money as well, calling it bills of credit.

Tensions between America and Britain continued to mount until the Revolutionary War broke out in 1775. The colonial leaders declared independence and created a new currency called Continentals to finance their side of the war. Unfortunately, each colony's government printed as much money as needed without backing it up by any standard or asset, so the Continentals experienced rapid inflation and became worthless. This discouraged the American government from using paper for almost a century.

The chaos from the Revolutionary War left the new nation's monetary system a complete wreck. Most of the currencies in the newly formed United States of America were useless. The problem wasn't resolved until 13 years later in 1788, when Congress was granted constitutional powers to coin money and regulate its value. Congress established a national monetary system and created the dollar as the currency unit of money. There was also a bimetallic standard, meaning that both silver and gold could be used to back paper dollars.

Eventually the US was ready to try the paper money experiment again. In the 1860s, the US government created more than $400 million in legal tender to finance its battle against the Confederacy in the American Civil War. These were called greenbacks because their backs were printed in green. The government backed this currency and stated that it could be used to pay back both public and private debts. The value did, however, fluctuate according to the North's success and failure at certain stages in the war. Confederate dollars, also issued by the seceding states during the 1860s, followed the fate of the Confederacy and were worthless by the end of the war.

In February 1863, the US Congress passed the National Bank Act. This act established a monetary system whereby national banks issued notes backed by US government bonds. Banknotes had been in circulation all the while, but because banks issued more notes than they had coin to cover, these notes often traded at less than face value. The US Treasury then worked to get state banknotes out of circulation so that the national banknotes would become the only currency.

During the period of Reconstruction, there was a lot of debate over the bimetallic standards. Some people were for using just silver to back the dollar, others were for gold. The situation was resolved in 1900 when the Gold Standard Act was passed, which made gold the sole backing for the dollar. This meant that, in theory, you could take your paper money and exchange it for the corresponding value in gold. In 1913, the Federal Reserve was created and given the power to steer the economy by controlling the money supply and interest rates on loans.

Modern Money: Forex and Bitcoin

It would not be fair to conclude this chapter without mentioning two of the latest developments in money management: *forex trading* and *virtual currency*.

The foreign exchange market, better known as forex, is the world's most traded market with turnover of $5.1 trillion per day. To put this into perspective, the U.S. stock market trades around $257 billion a day. That is quite a large sum, but only a fraction of what forex trades.

Forex is traded 24 hours a day, five days a week across banks, institutions, and individual traders worldwide. Unlike other financial markets, there is no centralized marketplace for forex, currencies trade over the counter in whatever market is open at that time.

Trading forex involves the buying of one currency and simultaneous selling another. In forex, traders attempt to profit from buying and selling currencies by actively speculating on the direction currencies are likely to take in the future.

Bitcoin is money in virtual form, known as cryptocurrency. It is a decentralized digital currency without a central bank or single administrator that can be sent from user to user on the peer-to-peer bitcoin network without the need for intermediaries.

Bitcoin can be bought and sold like any asset, but with no transaction charges and no need to identify yourself, making it a great option if you are a criminal or paranoid about government surveillance. As only a limited number were ever electronically "mined," it is considered to be an investment as well as a means of exchange.

However, it is held in digital wallets, which can be destroyed by a computer virus or failed disk. Digital exchanges like Mt. Gox have had problems with hacking and stolen bitcoins. There is no consumer protection for theft or other losses, unlike many real-world financial products. There is also the ever-present threat of government crack downs. China made virtual currencies illegal in 2007, and Western governments have expressed concern about its use in tax evasion and drug trafficking.

In summary, money has changed a lot since the days of shells and skins, but its main function hasn't changed at all. Regardless of what form it takes, money offers us a medium of exchange for goods and services and allows the economy to grow as transactions can be completed at greater speeds.

CHAPTER 2

Wealth building, A spiritual Principle

The United States of America needs a "spiritual awakening" regarding personal money management. I make this statement based on a recent research study which showed that the average American is saving less than 5% of their take-home income.

In addition to the research mentioned above, a 2017 research study showed that nearly 50% of all Americans did not have $500 in savings in the event of an emergency and almost 23% of Americans had less than $100 in savings. These research studies and statistics support the notion that a spiritual awakening regarding money management is much needed.

Let us look at the definition of spiritual awakening by Scott Jeffrey, an accomplished author on the subject of self-development. A spiritual awakening is an awakening of a dimension of reality beyond the confines of the ego. The ego is our exclusive sense of self, or "I". This awakening occurs when the ego somehow lets go so that a higher self or spirit can arise within.

As we deal with the concept of money and wealth-building as a spiritual principle, there are some foundational ideas that we must discuss and, in some instances, change, such as your mindset or beliefs.

10 Principles to Help Guide You on Your Journey to Understanding the Spiritual Side of Money

1. Money is not bad

Many of you have been taught that money is evil. However, this is not the case. Money is made by man. Man can be evil, but money cannot. Money is neither evil nor good. It is just an instrument to use and conduct business transactions, that is all. Basically, money is used for evil when it goes to evil people and money is used for good when it goes to good people.

If you desire money for good purposes in life, then money is not bad, it is going to make your life comfortable. The whole purpose of spiritualism is to make your life easy and happy. If you obtain a life of ease and happiness with money, then you are fulfilling the purpose of spirituality.

So, starting today, never say that money is bad or good. Just take it as an instrument to gain things in life. Make this your first spiritual principle of money.

2. Abundance Thinking

When we think about the financial condition of the world, we think about *scarcity*. However, if we view the world based on spiritual laws and principles, abundance is everywhere. If you are going to make money, never think that financial resources in the world are scarce. There are abundant opportunities to make money, so let abundance be your second spiritual principle.

3. Guilt of possessing money

Some spiritual teachings support the notion that the desire to obtain money is not good. As stated in the first principle, money is neither good nor bad. In fact, it is much needed to survive. If you are obtaining money for the right reasons, you should never feel guilty about the wealth you obtain. On the other hand, if you are making money through unscrupulous methods, then it is sure that you will get bad results. Don't feel guilty if you are earning money with honesty. Let this be your third principle regarding money.

4. Money is for you

You should commit this concept to memory: "money is for you and not you for money."

If you are living your life for money, you are making a mistake, because money is only a vehicle to go where you want to in your life. Use money as a vehicle to reach your destination. Spiritualism teaches you to seek help from scriptures to reach your final destination. That is your moksha, liberation, and enlightenment. If you understand this principle and add it to the others, then money will never dominate your life and you can live peacefully as you earn.

5. Money does not attract money

If you think that money attracts money, you are incorrect. It is a great *idea* that attracts money. If you have no money but you have a multi-million-dollar idea, then surely if you have the right mindset and knowledge, you will be a millionaire. It is not a "one-night gain-game!" It can take years to reach that point. There are lots of examples of people who had nothing when they started their business but an idea and basic knowledge about money. They became what they wanted to be with just that idea. It is similar to spirituality in that you are lacking in spirit when you go searching for it.

If you think that by going to church, mandir, or mosque, you become a spiritual person, then you are wrong. If that was all it took, then all of humanity would be spiritual. In reality, very few people obtain that level of understanding.

The same principles apply to *money mentality*. Most people have the wrong idea about money. They think that money attracts money, and if you have no money, then you cannot be rich. But this is not true. You need ideas to be rich. Let the principle of being rich without money motivate you to a higher level.

6. You are unique

First, understand that nature has made you unique. No two thumbs in this world are identical. No two leaves are identical. You as an individual are unique, and so is your relationship with money, so be yourself!

Some people feel satisfied with a little money, and some people are never satisfied, even if they have all the money in the world. The problem here is not money, but their mindset. Their mind is not under control. It is true that in today's sophisticated world, we cannot live without money. But money is not everything. Money is only a vehicle. If you believe that after making a million dollars you would be happy, then you are deluding yourself.

Similarly, if you feel that after getting spiritual enlightenment you would be the most contented person who ever lived, then you are a fool. Spiritualism is a vehicle to understand yourself deeply. Spiritualism is not your final destination. You, your true self, are the final destination.

So, use money as a vehicle to better understand yourself. For example, if you want to become a millionaire, then it should be your goal to become a millionaire. However, you must grasp the essence of this whole process as well. Understanding the process should be your top priority. What you become as a person after earning your millions should be your focus. This is one of the most important principles of spiritual money management.

7. There is no money shortcut

It is impossible to get spiritual enlightenment with one snap!

If you get a hold of a million dollars without any effort using a shortcut, then it is certain that you are going to lose it in the near future. The same is true of most lottery winners. In most cases, these people have zero financial knowledge. This is the reason why they believe in the lottery system. If they had financial knowledge, they would never participate in the lottery. It is just a game of luck.

A real entrepreneur with financial education never believes in luck. He believes in making his own luck. He understands to never attempt a shortcut.

8. This is not a competition

When it comes to spirituality, if you are in competition, you are not going to gain anything.

If you are religious, you are one of the majority of people who gather in places of worship to compete in the name of spiritualism. All of the religions of the world are in competition with each other. Most religions teach some variation of the basic concept of love. However, they are all in a race to attract more followers. True spiritualism is not a competitive game, it is an individual journey.

Obtaining money and financial success is dependent upon a particular mindset. The majority of people making money in today's society are not in competition but are in collaboration. They work together and support each other. "No competition!"

9. No possessiveness

If you are going to make money to hoard away from the world, then sooner or later somebody else will snatch it from you. If that is your mindset, you should work on changing it. You should focus on acquiring money for the service of mankind. If you adopt this mentality, then money will flock to you.

"You make money if you are generous."
– Robert Kiyosaki

10. Remembrance of death

As we discuss the spiritual principles of money, the topic of death cannot be neglected. A spiritual person has to keep death in the forefront of their mind. A spiritual person is aware that if they die a poor person, they will die feeling regretful. If you feel regret at the time of your death, then in your mind, your life was not a successful one. You have only one life to live and it is short, so don't waste it on trivial things.

If you want to be happy on your death bed, then start making money through honest means so that you will have a smile on your face at the time of your death.

CHAPTER 3

The Psychology of Money and Wealth Building

The American Psychology Association's annual surveys reveal that since 2008, money has been the number one stressor for most Americans.

The psychology of money is how our beliefs, expectations and feelings influence behavior, success, and disappointment. This means that financial success is an "inside job" and is more determined by what's between our ears and inside our hearts than what's on the outside. The psychology of money helps us to become more aware of our money scripts, how we may be sabotaging ourselves, and how we can re-write those scripts to create more success.

The psychology of money is not just about wealth. The same mindset that creates financial success also creates success in relationships, careers, health, and lifestyles.

Since money has so many powerful symbolic meanings such as security, freedom, power, ego, control, acceptance, rejection, etc., our early upbringing often creates strong emotions and irrational behavior. That's why despite the size of our portfolio, nest egg, or income, almost everyone has psychological challenges with money.

Researchers have determined that the psychological understanding of money begins after the age of four. In a research study, children around the age of four were asked the question, "Where does money come from?" The most popular answer was "Banks." Most children were not able to understand the relationship between working and earning wages. Their understanding was limited to their experience of visiting the bank with their parents.

By age seven or eight, the same children had grasped the understanding that their parents had to work to earn money. It was noted that at this age, children began to understand the concept of money based on the spending and saving patterns of their parents. In addition, many of the children had their first experience with money in the form of pocket money or an allowance.

It was noted in the research that middle-class parents tended to provide more structure and guidance with their children's allowance while poorer parents tended to give their children allowance with little or no guidance. In many instances, middle-class parents made their children earn their allowance by completing chores and household tasks.

You need to understand that the process of acquiring financial knowledge and developing attitudes toward money is known as financial socialization. This process usually begins at home. However, research has shown that many children reach adulthood without any idea what their parents earn or what savings they might have.

The lessons you teach your children regarding money will more than likely follow them for a lifetime. They will have a psychological effect on your child's attitude and behavior towards money as well as the lessons they will teach their children.

Prosperity Thinking

Lasting success and financial fulfillment are dependent upon *prosperity thinking* while reducing poverty and scarcity thinking. Two things you must do are to free your mind of negativity regarding obtaining money and reprogram your mind and attitude about the value of one dollar.

Freeing your mind often means changing the people that surround you and changing the company that you keep. Your relatives and close friends can either pull you up or drag you down both financially and emotionally. In many instances, you are better off walking alone or choosing new associates who share your same financial goals and aspirations.

In a 1960s study commonly called the "marshmallow experiment," researchers at Stanford presented nursery school children with a tray of goodies that contained marshmallows, pretzels, and cookies. Researchers told the kids to select one treat, and that if they ate it immediately, they wouldn't receive anymore, but if they waited only a few minutes, they'd receive another one. If they could delay their gratification, they'd double their candy. They observed the children until they were adults and learned that the ones who were able to delay their gratification achieved much more success in life than the ones who wanted instant gratification.

If you are a spender, you can't delay gratification. When cash is in front of you, you can't resist the urge to have it right now, even if you'd have more later, just like the marshmallow. That's why it doesn't bother you if you don't have savings in the bank. You're happy making purchases and enjoying them in the moment. It's worked out well for so long, you just stick with the habit. But if you realize that you're trending towards extreme spending then you're probably looking to kick the habit to the curb.

Money and Self-Esteem

Money can affect self-esteem, but basing self-esteem on external factors like your financial situation is risky. Our external circumstances can change wildly and unexpectedly. So, when your opinion of yourself is wrapped up in what you have or don't have, and you compare these externals to others, your self-esteem becomes very unstable. You become easily crushed. Money is one of those external factors that many of us latch onto for a sense of validation. Money can interact with our self-esteem in a variety of ways.

It is common for people living in poverty to experience low self-esteem. Being unable to afford food and other essentials can make people feel like they are failures. They may internalize negative stereotypes that they must be poor because they are incompetent and deeply flawed as people. This low self-esteem can lead to a lack of confidence and a sense of hopelessness.

Associating wealth and money with self-esteem can be problematic for a number of reasons. First, if you choose to pursue wealth in the name of self-esteem, you could make decisions in life that don't align with your passions, values, and goals. You will pursue a career because it will make you wealthy, even if you hate the job and find it boring, uninspiring, uncreative, and totally at odds with who you are as a person.

Second, if you end up losing money, say from a job loss or business failure, then you could lose all of your confidence. Obviously, it's completely normal to worry about money and paying bills in these kinds of situations, but you need strong, stable self-esteem in order to recover and get back on your feet.

Third, when you let money dictate how much you value yourself, you really won't value yourself very much. Deep down, we all want to feel that we have traits and qualities that give us a sense of self-esteem and confidence. But the amount of money in our bank account isn't enough to give us healthy self-esteem.

If you're on a low-income budget, this can affect your opinion of yourself when it comes to relationships. This is especially true of men who feel expected to pursue status, which they may associate with earning a lot of money. A man may view himself negatively or unattractive because he may not be able to afford an expensive apartment, car, holiday, or meal out.

For both genders, however, lacking the funds to buy certain things can impact self-esteem. It becomes a whole lot easier to date confidently and form a healthy relationship with someone else when your self-esteem is based on personal attributes.

Comparing Your Wealth to Others

Financially-based social comparison will trip you up. Stop comparing yourself to others! If you associate wealth with happiness, success, or virtue, then it can be tempting to compare yourself to friends, acquaintances, siblings, or other family members, and put yourself down if you're earning less than them.

Comparing yourself to others can get in the way of fully realizing your potential and expressing your very best qualities. For example, you may decide to pursue a career in the name of passion, regardless of how much you will earn. Yet even if you're passionate about what you do and it brings out in your best abilities and qualities, the fact that you earn less compared to others can make you doubt yourself. This is why it's important to value and appreciate your decisions, life choices, and personal achievements in and of themselves. Once you work on doing this, your self-esteem won't be so swayed by money and the lives of others.

The Value of a Dollar

Until you understand the value of one dollar, you will never be worth more tomorrow than you are today.

There is clearly a psychology behind the power of one dollar. It is when you focus on this power that you are ready to get on the road to wealth building. The question you must ask is, "How can I effectively maximize the use of one dollar?"

There is a psychology behind identifying your attitude and level of respect for the power of one dollar and money in general. When we talk about the psychology of money, we must include attitudes towards money. Your attitude plays a very important role in either attracting money to your life or driving it away.

If you grew up in an environment that undermined self-esteem and lacked motivation or ambition, it would be harder for you to attract money. If you believe that you don't deserve to be wealthy or believe money is filthy, then you probably feel that you don't deserve to have enough money, even if you consciously wish you had more.

With a negative attitude towards money, you will not put effort into earning it, you won't pay attention to opportunities, and you might make some errors of judgment that would cause you to lose money. On the other hand, if your attitude is positive, and you are open and willing to have wealth, you will attract money into your life in various ways.

It is funny to hear people say how much they want money and wish they had more, yet in the deep recesses of their subconscious mind, where it counts most, they repel any opportunity to improve their situation. It is difficult to attract money if there is a negative attitude about it. You cannot attract something that deep in your heart you despise. This is a common attitude for many people. They desire money, but their attitude is negative and therefore repellent.

If you want to attract money, you have to first get rid of all the negative thoughts and attitudes about it. A years-long bad habit has to change.

Changing Your Attitude

There are many techniques that can help you change your attitude about money and one of them is the technique of repeating affirmations.

By repeating affirmations aimed at changing your attitude towards money, your subconscious mind will eventually accept them as true and a negative attitude will gradually be replaced by a positive attitude.

Below are a few affirmations for achieving a positive attitude towards money:

- I deserve to possess money
- I have the right to have money
- Money is a useful tool
- Money can improve my life
- I am very comfortable with having money in my account
- Money is flowing into my life in harmonious ways

Affirmations can help you focus your mind on money and motivation, and inspire you to act. They help you become more aware of opportunities to make money.

The million-dollar question is, "What is holding many people back from earning and having more money?" It is usually one or both of the following reasons:

1. They feel that they do not deserve to have money. This might be due to their life experiences, education, upbringing, or lack of self-esteem.
2. The don't believe that they can make more money, have a better job, or progress in their job.

Some people are afraid to take the necessary steps to make more money. They avoid risks or starting new projects, and prefer to stay with the same job even though the pay is low.

If you keep thinking negative thoughts and fill your mind with worries and fears, you do not let anything positive happen in your life. In this way you prevent money from coming to you. If you keep focusing on your current financial situation, you keep recreating the same situation. Instead, you need to focus on how you want your financial condition to be. The real "magic" of affirmations is not repeating meaningless words but repeating them in such a way that they motivate you to take action, inspire you, and open your eyes to recognize opportunities.

To make affirmations work, you need to affirm with faith that what you are saying is already true. Just repeating the words with no faith or belief and hoping for a miracle is not enough.

Finally, do not lose hope if you do not achieve immediate results. It takes time to erase negative thoughts about money. That's why you need to keep affirming until you get results.

Forgiveness

One of the first steps that must be taken to change your mindset towards money is the practice of *self-forgiveness*.

Forgiveness is a powerful tool because it prevents us from being a prisoner of our past. If we shift our focus away from shame, we can make room for better practices and a healthier attitude towards money. It's important to acknowledge and accept what has happened. Make your apologies to yourself and those around you where necessary and focus on moving forward. Your financial mistakes are not you; your self-worth is independent of your mistakes.

It is important to become familiar with your mindset. We make many money decisions on a daily basis. It is a good idea to track your thoughts each time you make a financial decision. Take one or two days and write down what you were thinking each time you made a financial decision or transaction. This will deepen your awareness of your attitude towards money. With more clarity about your mindset, you can identify beliefs and habits that affect your ability to stick to goals.

Money, Culture, and Ethnicity

As we continue to discuss the psychology of money, it is impossible not to discuss the variations and cultural perspectives among different ethnic groups.

We should first look at a recent study regarding just how long a dollar circulates in various communities. Below is a timetable:

- The Asian Community   30 days
- Jewish Community   20 days
- White Community   17 days
- Black Community   6 hours

I am sure you can draw many conclusions regarding the psychological state of mind of each group as it relates to money and impulse spending. Now let us take a closer look at the cultural variations that affect attitudes towards money.

In Asian cultures a high degree of respect is given to money, but the ultimate motivation comes from a spiritual feeling of fate and self-denial. Asians typically view money as a necessity, needed to eat and to live. Most Asian cultures are non-verbal in their social dealings. The culture as a whole values hard work, but that work must be in harmony with life and nature. To that end, one typically earns money to survive and enjoy collective family goals.

There are four major concepts that dominate the Chinese attitude towards money. Let us take a brief look at these four concepts:

1.   Being frugal is a virtue

In Chinese culture, the concept of frugality has been taught for thousands of years. The classic Chinese text Dao De Jing states that the three greatest treasures one can have are love, frugality, and generosity. Frugality is really an integral part of the Chinese culture.

2.   Saving as much as possible

The personal savings rate in China is incredibly high compared to the United States. According to a 2006 CNN article, the personal savings rate of Chinese households was 30% and some Chinese households saved as much as 50% to 60%.

3.   Pay for things in cash

Credit cards are still rare in China and most people pay for everything in cash. It is only recently that the Chinese government allowed home ownership. Many Chinese teachers and factory workers were able to withdraw savings equivalent to ten to twenty times their annual salaries to pay for their homes in cash. Most Chinese people are wary of debt.

4. Always look for a bargain

For most Chinese, haggling is a way of life. The bargaining behavior of many Chinese have caused them to bear the stereotype of "cheap-skates" in America.

Let us now turn our focus to Hispanic culture. At 17% of the current population according to February 2019 statistics, Hispanics are now the largest minority group in America. Recent research shows that most Hispanics have a greater stability with their day-to-day finances than most other ethnic groups. This is a result of their abilities to save and maintain employment. While they are more likely to spend their income on appliances, gadgets, furniture, and entertainment, they are less likely to spend on vacations, life insurance, and basic medical services. The majority of Hispanics do not use credit cards. They are more likely to lend and borrow among family members. Unfortunately, most Hispanics do not put money aside for retirement.

Let us now take a look at the psychology behind the attitude towards money in the African American community. There are many issues that complicate this subject, but we will address a few. At the root of the problem is the fact that the majority of African Americans do not have a budget nor any idea as to where their money goes. Another major issue is it is often a common practice within the African American community to loan money to family and friends instead of saving or paying down debts. Unfortunately, the majority of African Americans live from paycheck to paycheck with no emergency fund or savings. In many instances, African Americans pile on credit card debt without knowing their credit score.

Although this is not an ethnic group, I think it is important to take a look at the LGBTQ community. In a recent survey of LGBTQ Americans, nearly 50% of all respondents stated that they struggled to maintain adequate savings. This percentage is higher than that of the non-LGBTQ community.

In addition, more than one-third of the respondents admitted that they had bad spending habits that need improvement. Over 50% of respondents admitted that the primary contributing factor to overspending was dining out. Dining out and socializing is a major part of LGBTQ culture.

Right behind dining out was the purchase of clothing. Almost 40% of those in the survey stated that they overspend when purchasing clothes. Lastly, more than one in four stated that they overspend on personal hygiene goods and services.

We conclude this topic with a look at the most dominate group throughout the history of America, the white community.

It is important to enlighten you regarding historical business practices especially as they relate to the treatment of African Americans by white America. Whites have benefited for decades from a vast wealth gap driven by segregation, redlining, evictions, and exclusion. These business practices have perpetuated the income and wealth gap in America.

Recent research statistics show that the probability of a loan denial is 36.9% higher for black-owned businesses than for white-owned businesses. On average, Hispanics pay 2.45% higher interest rates on loans than whites do. A survey that was conducted between 1998 and 2003 found that racial discrimination takes place among all minority groups as it relates to small business financing.

In 2013, the medium net worth of African American households was $11,000. For Latino households it was $13,700. At the same time, the medium net worth of the average white household was $141,000. In late 2016, the homeownership rate for white households was 72%, while it was less than 42% for blacks and 46% for Latino households.

The question at the center of this discussion that needs to be answered is, "Do white people have a healthy attitude towards money?" The second question is, "Does their financial success result from advantages in life or simply hard work?" Could it be a combination of the two?

The divide on this answer can be observed within political affiliations, i.e. Democrats verses Republicans. In a recent poll 56% of Republicans cited "lack of effort" as the primary reason for the wealth gap while only 19% of Democrats agreed with them. Meanwhile, 71% of Democrats blamed "circumstances beyond their control" as the root problem, while only 32% of Republicans agreed with them.

As I draw my own conclusions regarding the attitude of whites towards money and wealth building, I conclude that it is a combination of both advantages in life and hard work. I think it is unfair to focus on just the advantages that most whites have enjoyed from generation to generation. Even though it is no secret that many white businessmen participate in unscrupulous business practices, they must still be recognized for work ethic.

Naturally, there are many reasons why whites have maintained their current dominant financial position from one generation to the next. One of the primary reasons is that they continue to pass their wealth down through generations. However, there are other factors like education level and caliber of schools that their children attend.

The economic values that they instill within their children by example such as better houses, neighborhoods, and automobiles has an impact on their children's attitude towards money. It is a common practice to give their children allowances at a very young age to teach them money concepts early on. As they grow, establishing an educational fund further perpetuates their children's disposition towards the importance of money. All of these factors help to establish a higher self-esteem and ultimately a more positive attitude towards money and the accumulation of wealth.

Let me summarize this chapter regarding the psychology of money with these words. The understanding and attitude towards money begins at the cradle and ends with the grave. You are never too young or too old to change your paradigm as it relates to the importance of money, its necessity, and its value.

What separates animals from human beings is that animals function by instincts and human beings by reasoning. Animals are limited in their ability to change behavior. However, humans can change at will if they are motivated and desire to do so.

When you consider your spending habits and attitude towards money, try to remember these words: The temporary joy and satisfaction that you receive when spending will never equate to the pain you will endure if you retire with no assets and personal wealth. It is not until you reach your death bed that you will take inventory of your life and how you handled your personal finances.

CHAPTER 4

Wealth around the World

Many people believe that the US is the richest country in the world. However, recent statistics show that the US didn't even make the top ten in comparison to other rich countries around the world. We will begin our discussion on the subject of wealth around the world with a look at the top ten countries that dominate the world economy and offer its citizens the highest standard of living. This research is based on each country's most recent reported GDP.

The Wealthiest Countries in the World

The US is the eleventh richest country, just missing the top ten. The US GDP per capita is estimated at $59,500, falling just short of the Republic of San Marino which came in with a per capita GDP of $60,360. Many economists say that this is still impressive because the US currently has the world's largest economy, with a population of over 310 million people.

WEALTH AROUND THE WORLD

The top ten richest countries are as follows.

10. San Marino

The tiny European microstate of San Marino holds the designation of being the world's 10th richest country, with the average personal income coming in at $60,360 (USD). Major industries in San Marino include banking, tourism, electronics, and wine and cheese production. Notably, San Marino holds no national debt.

9. Switzerland

The GDP per Swiss citizen is $61,360. Swiss banking and financial institutions keep the country and its economy afloat. It is important to note that some of the wealthiest people and companies in the world own Swiss bank accounts, and therefore Switzerland has excess capital to use for investment purposes. Zurich and Geneva, Switzerland's most well-known cities, have consistently ranked among the top ten world-wide in terms of standards of living.

8. The United Arab Emirates

This Middle Eastern federation of emirates has a land area of about 32,278 sq. miles, which means it could easily fit within New York State (54,556 sq. miles). With a population of 9.2 million people, it's a bit more populated than the state of New Jersey. Roughly one third of the $68,250 GDP per capita economy comes from oil revenues, while the service and telecommunications sectors also contribute significantly. The UAE is the second largest economy in the Arab world after Saudi Arabia.

... 33 ...

7. Kuwait

Kuwait hosts a small, relatively open economy and its citizens enjoy a per capita GDP of $69,670. The highest-valued currency unit in the world is currently the Kuwait dinar. With nearly 10% of the world's oil reserves, petroleum accounts for nearly half of the GDP and 95% of export revenues and government income.

6. Norway

This Nordic nation's per capita GDP of $70,590 allows its 4.97 million people to reap the benefits of a small yet robust economy. Driven by fishing, natural resources, and major petroleum exploration, Norway is the 8th largest exporter of crude oil, 9th largest exporter of refined oil, and 3rd largest exporter of natural gas in the world. Norway also consistently ranks among the world's best places to live.

5. Ireland

The Emerald Isle has a per capita income of about $72,630 with a population of about 4.8 million people. The main industries that boost its economy are textiles, mining, and food production – staple products in any economy. In OECD (Organization of Economic Cooperation and Development) rankings, Ireland actually places 4th overall.

4. Brunei

With a per capita income of $76,740, Brunei ranks as the 4th richest country in the world. This tiny state in Southwest Asia has a total area of 2,226 sq. miles and a population of 417,200 as of July 2015. The country's wealthy economy is supported by the petroleum sector. Brunei is the 9th largest producer of liquified natural gas in the world as well as the 3rd largest oil producer in Southeast Asia.

3. Singapore

This tiny city-state has moved up from 5th position to take 3rd with a per capita income of $90,530. That is five times the average per capita income for the ordinary individual in the world. The basis of Singapore's wealth is its financial services sector, a chemical export industry, and its liberal economic policies that encourage growth and innovation. Singapore has the 2nd busiest port in the world, exporting $414 billion in goods in 2011 alone.

2. Luxembourg

A symbol of wealth, Luxembourg takes 2nd place with a per capita GDP of $109,190. This is nine times the world average. The backbone of this economy is its vibrant financial sector, prudent fiscal policies, and dynamic industrial and steel sectors. Banking in Luxembourg is the largest sector of its economy with an asset base of over $1.24 trillion alone.

1. Qatar

Recent research data confirms that Qatar is the richest country in the world, with a per capita income of $124,930. Qatar has a well-developed oil exploration industry. Petroleum accounts for 70% of its government revenues, 60% of its GDP, and 85% of its export earnings.

Now that we have taken a look at the top ten richest countries in the world based on GDP per capita, let us take a look at the world's top ten economies by GDP. Gross Domestic Product (GDP) is the monetary value of all finished goods and services a country generates in a specific time frame. It is the most common measure of economic output and strength. Virtually all countries around the world measure and report their GDP on a regular basis. This allows us to directly compare their economic power. Fortunately, the World Bank provides a comprehensive database of economic indicators, including current and historical data on GDP for most countries.

The top ten economies in the world are as follows:

10. Canada

The world's 10th largest economy according to GDP is Canada, with an official GDP of $1.5 trillion (USD) in 2016. The country has strong industries in transportation equipment, chemicals, food products, wood and paper products, as well as fishing. If we look at the composition of GDP by sector of origin, the services sector is responsible for about 70.2% of the country's GDP, followed by industry (28.1%) and agriculture (1.7%). Like most countries, Canada has seen a huge increase in GDP over the last 50 years: in 1960 it was reported at just $40.46 billion.

9.   Brazil

The next country on the list is Brazil, with an official GDP of $1.7 trillion. The country is known for its textile and shoe industry as well as strong cement, lumber, iron ore, and tin industries. Brazil also boasts a relatively strong agriculture sector, which makes up about 6% of the total GDP. However, as in most modern economies, the service (72.8%) and industrial (21%) sectors still account for most of the country's GDP. Brazil is still recovering from a strong recession in 2015 and 2016. Before the recession, the country's economic output was reported significantly higher at almost $2.5 trillion in 2013 and 2014.

8.   Italy

With an official GDP of $1.86 trillion, Italy is the world's 8th largest economy. In addition, it is the 4th largest economy in the eurozone. The country's major industries include tourism, machinery, iron and steel, chemicals, clothing, and food processing. As a result, the services sector (73.9%) and the industrial sector (24%) together make up about 98% of the total GDP.

7. India

Next in line is India. India's official GDP is estimated at $2.26 trillion. The country has a diverse economy, with strong industries like textiles, chemicals, steel, mining, machinery, pharmaceuticals, and software. Due to its large rural areas, the country's agricultural sector makes up about 16.8% of the total GDP. The industrial sector accounts for 28.9% and services for the remaining 46.6%. In recent years, India has developed into an open-market economy which has accelerated the country's growth.

6. France

The world's 6th largest economy is France, with a GDP of $2.47 trillion. It is also the 3rd largest economy in the eurozone. The country's strongest industries include machinery, chemicals, automobiles, aircraft, electronics, and tourism. The services sector accounts for 78.9% of total GDP, followed by the industrial sector (19.4%) and the agriculture sector (1.6%). France has committed to a form of capitalism that maintains social equity by means of the law. As a result, the government still maintains a relatively strong presence in the economy.

5. United Kingdom (UK)

Number five on the list is the United Kingdom (UK), with a GDP of $2.65 trillion. The UK is also the 2nd largest economy in Europe. The most important industries in the UK include machine tools, electric power equipment, shipbuilding, aircraft manufacturing, chemicals, food processing, clothing, and other consumer goods. The economy has a strong services sector, which makes up 80.4% of the country's GDP. The industrial sector accounts for 19% and agriculture just 0.6%. The UK was hit hard during the 2008 financial crisis. Although it has recovered quite well since then, it has seen another economic downturn in 2015 and 2016.

4. Germany

The world's 4th largest economy by GDP is Germany, with an official GDP of $3.48 trillion. Germany is also the most powerful economy in the eurozone. It is among the world's largest producers of iron, steel, coal, chemicals, machinery, automobiles, and machine tools. Nevertheless, the country's strongest sector is the services sector, which accounts for 69.3% of total GDP. The industrial sector accounts for 30.1%, while the agriculture sector only adds the remaining 0.6%.

3. Japan

With a GDP of $4.95 trillion, Japan is the world's 3rd most powerful economy. It ranks among the world's largest and most technologically advanced producers of motor vehicles, machine tools, electronics, ships, chemicals, and processed foods. The most dominant sector in Japan is the services sector, which is responsible for 70.9% of the country's total GDP. The industrial sector makes up 29.7% and the agriculture sector accounts for the remaining 1%. Japan's position as one of the world's strongest economies is impressive, especially because the country is scarce in critical natural resources.

2. China

The 2nd largest economy in the world is China, with an official GDP of $11.2 trillion in 2016. China is also the world's largest country by population, with more than 1.3 billion people. It is the world leader in industrial output and dominates mining, iron, steel, aluminum, machine building, textiles and apparel, chemicals, as well as consumer products. This results in a strong industrial sector, which accounts for 39.5% of total GDP. Services accounts for 52.2%, and agriculture for 8.2% of the country's GDP. It is important to note that 40 years ago, China was a closed, centrally planned economy. Since then it has developed into one of the world's leading economic powers.

1. United States

The world's most powerful economy is the United States with a GDP of $18.6 trillion. The US also has the most technologically advanced economy in the world with highly diversified industries like petroleum, steel, motor vehicles, aerospace, chemicals, electronics, food process-ing, and consumer goods. The most important sector in the US is the services sector, which accounts for 80.2% of total GDP, followed by the industrial sector (18.9%) and agriculture (0.9%). Despite increasing pressure from low-wage producers such as China, the US has managed to consistently increase economic output over the last few years.

The Poorest Countries in the World

Now that we have taken a close look at the world's wealthiest coun-tries and economies, let us take a step back and look at the world's poorest countries.

I think it is very important to note that while there are enough re-sources in the world to take care of the whole of humanity, billions of people from poor countries are grappling with a humanitarian crisis. The 2019 estimate of poverty in the world puts 4 billion people below the poverty line. The big cause of this crisis is human-designed wars and corruption.

Of the 10 poorest countries in the world, most if not all of the people of each country exist on less than $2/day.

10. Yemen

The ongoing civil war in Yemen is causing massive damages to the economy. It's the worst humanitarian crisis of the decade. The beat down on the economy has seen the country's GDP per capita reduced to estimated $913 in 2019. Yemen suffers from a lack of infrastructure and resources such as water and healthcare. Most hospitals and roads have been damaged in the war. Many Yemenis have been displaced from their homes and businesses. They are currently facing an ongoing famine: approximately 14 million people face starvation, roughly one half of the population.

9. Mozambique

Mozambique's 2019 GDP per capita is the second lowest in the world at $502. Mozambique's economy is reliant upon agriculture, but without the use of modern agricultural engineering technology. Of the 15 million people who live in Mozambique, 12 million survive on less than $1.25/day. The main problem is crop failures due to bad weather and a lack of modern agricultural technology. In addition, diseases causing the death of parents and guardians leave a large dependent population.

8. Madagascar

Madagascar (most noted for its wildlife, especially penguins) is the fourth largest island in the world but it has not managed to unshackle itself from the chains of poverty. Most locals mainly depend on small-scale subsistence farming. The economy is battered by worsening climate conditions, resulting in destructive cyclones and monsoons, which cause loss of life and up to $250 million in destruction. In addition, they suffer from a lack of stable government. They have experienced many coups since breaking away from French rule. They currently have a $9.98 billion economy with an average of 64% of the population living below $1.00/day.

7. Malawi

Malawi is among the smallest countries in Africa but with a large population of 18 million. Although Malawi has enjoyed a peaceful and stable government since its independence, it falls on the list because bad weather and reliance on antiquated farming methods have led to food shortages. Diseases such as HIV causes families to sell their properties to provide healthcare for family members. The population of Malawi has a high level of illiteracy. Only about 66% of the people can read and write. The current ratio of doctors to patients is 1:50,000.

6. The Democratic Republic of Congo

While the Democratic Republic of Congo is well known for its vast natural resources, this country is on the list primarily as a result of corruption. The proceeds from the mines mainly fund genocidal warlords. The lack of infrastructure such as poor roads lead to huge transport costs, and farmers' produce does not reach the market easily. The current farming methods are antiquated. There is a lack of investment to stimulate the economy as a result of ongoing civil unrest. Lastly, rampant diseases such as malaria, cholera, and HIV have taken a toll on the labor force.

5. Burundi

From ethnic conflicts between the Hutu and the Tutsi to the present political crisis, the country's economy stands no chance of stabilizing. The main reason Burundi is on the list is because the European Union stopped the flow of aid in 2016, not to resume until the Burundian government adopts good governmental practices. The second reason is the government stopped trading with neighboring Rwanda, leading to rocketing food prices. Burundi has also seen a decrease in coffee production, which is the country's main export. Approximately 83% of the population survives on less than $1.25/day.

4.   South Sudan

South Sudan is near the top of the list of poorest countries primarily due to the greed of those in power and an ongoing war. About 400,000 people have died since the war broke out in 2013. Most of the proceeds from its economy go into military expenditures. South Sudan has the third highest military spending in the world. It depends on oil, but unfortunately, the production and exportation of oil has been hindered. Most Sudanese are destined to become peasant farmers. The average person in South Sudan lives off less than $3/day.

3.   The Central African Republic

The Central African Republic is the third poorest country in the world, with millions going without access to basic services such as food, healthcare, shelter, and clothing. The number one contributor to the country's poverty is diseases such as AIDS, which take away the family's breadwinners. An ongoing civil war and a huge debt has also hindered the economy. Roughly 64% of the 5 million people live below the poverty line.

2.   Liberia

The number one factor causing Liberia to rank second among the poorest countries was the 2014 Ebola epidemic, which led to a decline in productivity in agriculture, trade, and labor. Most Liberians lack basic infrastructures such as roads, electricity supply, water, and access to healthcare. Lastly, Liberia has a heavy dependence on foreign aid. Fifty-four percent of the 4.5 million people survive on less than $2.00/day.

1. Somalia

Somalia is the poorest country in the world. Among the top reasons contributing to the current economic condition is political instability and corruption by dictatorial regimes. Somalia is currently engaged in civil and ethnic wars. Lastly, severe climatic conditions also contribute to economic instability. Many Somalians are forced to live on less than $1.00/day.

What is it That Makes a Country Rich or Poor?

Now that we have shared with you the 10 richest and poorest countries, let us now try to explain why some countries are so rich while others continue to remain poor.

> *"Open markets offer the only realistic hope of pulling billions*
> *of people in developing countries out of abject poverty, while*
> *sustaining prosperity in the industrialized world."*
> **–Kofi Annan**

Many people mark the birth of economics with the publication of Adam Smith's *The Wealth of Nations* in 1776. Actually, this classic's full title is *An Inquiry into the Nature and Causes of the Wealth of Nations*, and Smith does indeed attempt to explain why some nations achieve wealth and others fail to do so. Yet, in the 241 years since the book's publication, the gap between rich countries and poor countries has grown even larger. Economists are still refining their answer to the original question: Why are some countries rich and others poor, and what can be done about it?

In common language, the terms *rich* and *poor* are often used in a relative sense: A poor person has less income, wealth, goods, or services than a rich person. When considering nations, economists often use gross domestic product (GDP) per capita as an indicator of average economic well-being within a country. GDP is the total market value, expressed in dollars, of all final goods and services produced in an economy in a given year. In a sense, a country's GDP is like its yearly income. So, dividing a particular country's GDP by its population is an estimate of how much income, on average, the economy produces per person (per capita) per year. In other words, GDP per capita is a measure of a nation's *standard of living*. For example, in 2016, GDP per capita was $57,467 in the United States, $42,158 in Canada, $27,539 in South Korea, $8,123 in China, $1,513 in Ghana, and $455 in Liberia.

Because GDP per capita is simply GDP divided by the population, it is a measure of income as if it were divided equally among the population. In reality, there can be large differences in the incomes of people within a country. So, even in a country with relatively low GDP, some people will be better off than others. And there are poor people in very wealthy countries. In 2013 (the most recent year comprehensive data on global poverty is available), 767 million people, or 10.7% of the world population, were estimated to be living below the international poverty line of $1.90 per person per day.

Whether for people or nations, the key to escaping poverty lies in rising levels of income. For nations specifically, which measure wealth in terms of GDP, escaping poverty requires increasing the amount of output per person that their economy produces. In short, economic growth enables countries to escape poverty.

Economic growth is a sustained rise over time in a nation's production of goods and services. How can a country increase its production?

Well, an economy's production is a function of its inputs, or factors of production (natural resources, labor resources, and capital resources), and the productivity of those factors (specifically the productivity of labor and capital resources, which is called total factor productivity or TFP). Consider a shoe factory. Total shoe production is a function of the inputs (raw materials such as leather, labor supplied by workers, and capital resources, which are the tools and equipment in the factory), but it also depends on how skilled the workers are and how useful the equipment is.

Now, imagine two factories with the same number of workers. In the first factory, workers with basic skills move goods around with push carts, assemble goods with hand tools, and work at benches. In the second factory, highly trained workers use motorized forklifts to move pallets of goods and use power tools to assemble goods that move along a conveyer belt. Because the second factory has higher TFP, it will have higher output, earn greater income, and provide higher wages for its workers.

Similarly, for an entire country, higher TFP will result in a higher rate of economic growth. A higher rate of economic growth means more goods are produced per person, which creates higher incomes and enables more people to escape poverty at a faster rate. But, how can nations increase TFP to escape poverty? While there are many factors to consider, two stand out.

First, institutions matter. For an economist, institutions are the *rules of the game* that create the incentives for people and businesses. For example, when people are able to earn a profit from their work or business, they have an incentive not only to produce but also to continually improve their *method* of production. The rules of the game help determine the economic incentive to produce. On the flip side, if people are not monetarily rewarded for their work or business, or if the benefits of their production are likely to be taken away or lost, the incentive to produce will diminish. For this reason, many economists suggest that institutions such as property rights, free and open markets, and the rule of law provide the best incentives and opportunities for individuals to produce goods and services.

Property Rights

Property rights refers to the ability of people to produce, buy, and sell goods and services and to profit from business ventures. The right to own private property also includes the ability to sell that property. Without secure property rights, not many people would be willing to start a business, buy a house or land, or invest.

Free and Open Markets

Free and open markets refer to the ability of people and businesses to buy and sell goods and services with minimal interference by governments. This is a balancing act because governments must provide protection for its citizens through regulation, but too much regulation can make economic transactions unprofitable and unattractive.

Rule of Law

Rule of law holds that the law and not individual government leaders govern the nation, and that government, its leaders, and citizens, must follow and obey the law. The rule of law provides a sense of stability and certainty for economic transactions. For example, people and businesses are more likely to invest for the future if they feel confident that the rules of the game are constant, rather than in a state of constant change.

North and South Korea serve as an example of the importance of institutions. In a sense they are a natural experiment. These two nations share a common history, culture, and ethnicity. In 1953 these nations were formally divided and governed by very different regimes. North Korea is a dictatorial communist nation where property rights and free and open markets are largely absent, and the rule of law is repressed. In South Korea, institutions provide strong incentives for innovation and productivity. The results? North Korea is among the poorest nations in the world, while South Korea is among the richest.

While this seems like a simple relationship—if government provides strong property rights, free markets, and the rule of law, markets will thrive, and the economy will grow—research suggests that the institution story alone does not provide a complete picture. In some cases, government support is important to the development of a nation's economy. Closer inspection shows that the economic transformation in South Korea, which started in the 1960s, was under the dictatorial rule of Park Chung-hee, who redirected the nation's economic focus on export-driven industry without strong property rights, free markets, and the rule of law, which came later. South Korea's move toward industrialization was an important first step in its economic development.

China is another example of an economy that has grown dramatically. In a single generation it has been transformed from a backward agrarian nation into a manufacturing powerhouse. China tried market reforms during the Qing dynasty (whose modernization reforms started in 1860 and lasted until its overthrow in 1911) and the Republic Era (1912-1949), but they were not effective. China's economic transformation began in 1978 under Deng Xiaoping, who imposed a government-led initiative to support industrialization and the development of commercial markets both internally and for export of Chinese goods. These early government-supported changes helped develop the markets necessary for the current dramatic increase in economic growth.

Second, international trade is an important part of the economic growth story for most countries. Think about two kids in the school cafeteria trading a granola bar for a chocolate chip cookie. They are willing to trade because it offers them both an opportunity to benefit. Nations trade for the same reason. When poorer nations use trade to access capital goods such as advanced technology and equipment, they can increase their TFP, resulting in a higher rate of economic growth. Trade provides a broader market for a country to sell the goods and services it produces. Many nations, however, have trade barriers that restrict their access to trade. Recent research suggests that the removal of trade barriers could close the income gap between rich and poor countries by 50%.

Economic growth of less-developed economies is key to closing the gap between rich and poor countries. Differences in the economic growth rate of nations often come down to differences in inputs (factors of production) and differences in TFP—the productivity of labor and capital resources. Higher productivity promotes faster economic growth, and faster growth allows a nation to escape poverty. Factors that can increase productivity and growth include institutions that provide incentives for innovation and production. In some cases, government can play an important part in the development of a nation's economy. Finally, increasing access to international trade can provide markets for the goods produced by less-developed countries and increase productivity by increasing the access to capital resources.

CHAPTER 5

Wealth in America

When we talk about wealth in America, it is very important to note that the richest 1% of the population now controls more of the country's wealth than at any time in the past 50 years.

When we define wealth in America, we must note that it is commonly measured in terms of *net worth*, which is the sum of assets minus liabilities. It is based on what you actually own and not how much you earn. According to a 2017 research paper by economist Edward N. Wolff, a federal survey of consumer finances revealed that the wealthiest 1% of American households own 40% of the country's wealth. That share is higher than it has ever been at any point since 1962.

Since 2013 the share of wealth owned by the 1% shot up by nearly three percentage points. Wealth owned by the bottom 90%, meanwhile, fell over the same period. Today, the top 1% of households own more wealth than the bottom 90% combined. The gap between the ultrawealthy and everyone else has only become wider in the past several decades.

In addition, the top 20% of households own 90% of the wealth. This leaves just 10% of the remaining wealth to be shared by 80% of the population. I think it is important to note that a recent study published by the Institute for Policy Studies using Forbes data concluded that the three richest Americans currently control more wealth than the total bottom 50% of the country. Those three individuals, Bill Gates, Warren Buffett, and Jeff Bezos collectively control more wealth that 160 million people or 63 million households. Roughly a fifth of Americans have zero or negative net worth.

Bezos, Gates, and Buffett held a combined fortune of $248.5 billion according to the 2017 *Forbes 400*. Since then, that figure has risen to an estimated $263 billion, thanks largely to Bezos, whose net worth has jumped more than $13 billion as a result of a surge in Amazon's share price. If left unchecked, wealth will continue to accumulate into fewer and fewer hands, following a decades-long trend.

Although the number of wealthy people in America is getting smaller as the ultra-rich get richer, it is important to note that according to the Spectrum Group's 2019 Market Insight report, there were 9.8 million individuals with a net worth between $1 million and $5 million, 1.8 million individuals with net worth between $5 and $25 million, and 156,000 households with more than $25 million net worth. In other words, there are roughly 11.8 million millionaires in America, making up roughly 3% of the population. This record represents an all-time high thanks to a bull market in stocks, bonds, and real estate.

A recent study shows that the more education you receive, the higher your chance of becoming a millionaire across all races. This makes sense because the higher paying jobs often require higher levels of education. However, for Asians with a bachelor's degree, the probability of millionaire status is roughly 17%, while for Hispanics with a master's degree, the chance for millionaire status is roughly 11%. The statistic that jumps out the most is the 37% probability a white person with a master's degree will become a millionaire. Thirty-seven percent is incredibly high compared to most other ethnic groups.

Unfortunately, the greatest surprise that the study revealed was the very low probability for Hispanics and blacks to become millionaires even with a master's degree. You would think that by the time you get to the master's level of education that the people and institutions you are affiliated with would provide very similar financial and career opportunities for all ethnic groups. However, for blacks with a master's degree, only 7% have a chance of becoming a millionaire. Something seems very wrong with this scenario.

According to data from the Federal Reserve Board's survey of consumer finance, the odds of becoming a millionaire in America are 6.4% to 22.3%. These are greater odds than in almost every other country in the world. For example, the chances of becoming a millionaire in Zambia are less than 1%.

On average, individuals who become financially literate and consult personal finance websites have a 60% greater chance of becoming a millionaire. This is three times higher than the chance of anyone in America who does not understand basic financial concepts.

The reasoning behind this is that seeking personal finance resources will often cause you to pay more attention to your finances. As soon as you have a heightened awareness about how much you are saving, what you are investing, your net worth asset allocation, and your retirement plan, it's only natural to generate more wealth than the typical person who is financially unaware.

If you put away just $350 a month and earn 6% interest per year, you will become a millionaire in 46 years. If you decide to wisely max out your 401K at $1,500 a month and earn 7.5% per year, you will become a millionaire in just 22 years. And if you decide to max your 401K and invest another $1,000 in after-tax proceeds a month, you will become a millionaire in just 17 years if you earn 7.5% in interest per year.

The Racial Wealth Gap

The racial wealth gap in the United States is the disparity in median household wealth between the different races. This gap is most pronounced between white households and racial minorities. Whites have more wealth than black, Latino, and Native-American households.

A 2018 survey found that whites severely underestimate the racial wealth gap. They think that black wealth is about 80% that of whites. Data from the US Census Bureau reveals that black wealth is about 9% that of whites.

In 2016, the median net worth of non-Hispanic white households was $143,600. The median net worth of black households was $12,920 and $21,420 for Hispanic households. Native American wealth has not even been measured since 2000. At that time, their median household net worth was just $5,700.

In contrast, Asian American households have more wealth than white households. But that apparent success story hides a wealth gap within the minority. The richest Asian Americans held 168 times more wealth than the poorest Asian Americans. It's a greater disparity than that of white households, where the richest 10% owned 121 times more than the poorest 10%.

The gap is worsening. Between 1983 and 2013, white households saw their wealth increased by 14%. But during the same period, black household wealth declined 75%. Median Hispanic household wealth declined 50%.

One reason for the discrepancy is the number of extremely poor black families. The Economic Policy Institute reported that 25% of black households have zero or negative net worth. Only 10% of white families are that poor. Since so many black families own nothing or are in debt, it drags down average wealth for the entire race. As a result, black families have $5.04 in net worth for every $100 held by white families.

Education is also a powerful factor in improving economic mobility. Education increases the income that generates greater economic growth. Over a lifetime, Americans with college degrees earn 84% more than those with only high school degrees. A 2009 McKinsey study found that the average score of black and Hispanic students on standardized tests was two to three years behind that of white students of the same age.

This racial wealth gap exists even among blacks who are highly educated and come from two-parent homes. Black families with graduate or professional degrees have $200,000 less in wealth than similarly educated whites. Black or Latino college graduates don't even have as much wealth as white high school dropouts. Similarly, two-parent black households have less wealth than single-parent white households.

Until the 13th Amendment in 1865, slavery legally prevented blacks from building wealth. Until the Civil Rights Act of 1964, Jim Crow laws perpetuated segregation in the south. They detailed what jobs blacks could take and how much they could be paid. They created indentured servitude. They restricted where blacks lived and traveled. Public parks, transportation, and restaurants were segregated. Even some entire towns were off limits to blacks.

These laws were violently enforced by the Ku Klux Klan and lynchings. Between 1882 and 1968, 4,743 lynchings occurred in the United States, 3,446 of which were of black people. White mobs lynched blacks for some perceived breach of the racial hierarchy. Most of the lynchings took place in small southern towns where poor white farmers perceived blacks as an economic threat.

In 1935, the Social Security Act excluded farm workers and domestic workers from accruing benefits. At that time, most blacks still lived in the South and they were illiterate. That meant they were more likely to be farm workers and domestic workers. As a result, two-thirds of blacks never received Social Security's wealth-building opportunities. The mobilization for World War II and the civil rights movement sought to reverse this legal discrimination. It had mixed results.

In 1948, President Harry Truman ordered the military to be integrated. The G.I. Bill of Rights assisted veterans with housing, education, and jobs. Between 1944 and 1971, it distributed $95 billion in benefits. But it was left to the states to administer. As a result, black veterans in the South were denied access.

In 1954, the *Brown v. Board of Education* Supreme Court case ruled that school segregation was unconstitutional. But whom attended which school followed local neighborhood boundaries, and neighborhoods were segregated. In 1964, the Civil Rights Act ended Jim Crow laws. In 1965, the Voting Rights Act protected blacks' right to vote. In 1968, the Fair Housing Act ended legal discrimination in renting and selling homes.

The legacy of the Jim Crow laws created a structural inequality that's been difficult to erase. Despite these laws, discrimination against blacks owning wealth has continued. Welfare programs, such as the Transitional Assistance for Needy Families and the Supplemental

Nutrition Assistance Program, forbid beneficiaries from accumulating wealth. In some states, they can't save more than $1,000 or own cars worth more than $4,650.

Federal government policies actively promote wealth building. Each year, the federal government offers around $400 billion in tax cuts designed to build wealth, according to the Corporation for Enterprise Development. At least 34% of the cuts promote homeownership, while another third subsidizes savings and investment. A 2018 Duke University study reported that reducing the racial homeownership gap would narrow the racial wealth gap by 31%.

These tax cuts help the wealthy more than the poor. The wealthiest 5% of Americans are in the best financial position to take advantage of them. As a result, half of the $400 billion goes to that 5%. The middle 60% only receive 4% of these tax cuts. The bottom 20% of taxpayers get almost nothing.

Higher birth rates and immigration mean that minorities are becoming a larger share of the US population. By 2045, blacks and Latinos will outnumber whites. As a result, the racial wealth gap will drag down the average wealth of the entire country. Between 1983 and 2013, US median wealth has dropped from $78,000 to $64,000. White wealth has increased, but black and Latino median wealth has fallen.

It's also created an achievement gap between races. If there had been no achievement gap in the years between 1998 and 2008, US gross domestic product would have been $525 billion higher in 2008. Similarly, if low income students had the same educational achievement as their wealthier peers over that same period, they would have added $670 billion in GDP. A McKinsey study found that it's cost the US economy more than all recessions since the 1970s.

Closing the Gap

One way to close the gap is to increase economic mobility. Despite the promise of the American dream, the United States has lower levels of economic mobility than other developed countries.

Progressive taxation will help close the inequality in US income. Poor families spend a larger share of their income on the cost of living. They need all the money they earn to afford basics like shelter, food, and transportation. A tax cut would allow them to afford a decent standard of living. It would also allow them to start saving and increase their wealth.

Equity in education would bring everyone up to at least a minimum standard. Research shows that the greatest single correlation of high income is the education level of one's parents. Equity would allow minority children to be more competitive with those who live in higher-income school districts. It would give them stronger skills in the job market and in managing their finances. Investing in human capital is a better solution than increasing welfare benefits or providing a universal basic income.

One way to do this would be to establish Child Savings Accounts limited to education or homeownership. The accounts could grow tax-free and not penalize welfare recipients. In 2016, the Annie E. Casey Foundation found that a CSA program begun in 1979 would have completely closed the gap between whites and Latinos. The gap between whites and blacks would have shrunk by 82%.

A University of Michigan study found an inexpensive and effective method of delivering higher education to the poor. Researchers sent packets to hundreds of high-performing, low-income high school students in Michigan. They invited them to apply to the University and promised scholarships to pay for all costs. More than two-thirds applied to the university compared to 26% in a control group that didn't receive the packets.

Increasing income at the low end of the scale will give those workers an opportunity to save and build wealth. Between 1979 and 2007, income inequality destroyed Americans' economic mobility. Household income rose 65% for the top fifth, but just 18% for the bottom fifth. If public policy equalized income between blacks and whites, black wealth would grow $11,488 per household, shrinking the wealth gap by 11%. Similarly, median Latino wealth would grow $8,765, shrinking the wealth gap by 9%. One way to do this is to raise the minimum wage. Studies show that cities that have done so reduced poverty and reliance on welfare.

Professor William Darity, from the Samuel DuBois Cook Center on Social Equity at Duke University, suggests a baby bonds program. It would pay for a trust fund for the 4 million new children born in America each year. It would cost $100 billion or 2% of the federal budget. Children from poor families would receive more, while those from wealthy families would receive less. Beneficiaries would use it for education, home equity, or other investments when they turned 18. They could plan their lives knowing this fund was available.

The program would generate more revenue for the government through higher income taxes. It would also generate more revenue for local communities through higher property taxes.

To reduce the racial wealth gap, politicians must stop pretending that trickle-down economics works. The Tax Policy Center showed that Trump's 2017 Tax Cut and Jobs Act would give families earning $25,000 or less annually a $40 tax cut. It would give those earning $3.4 million annually a $940,000 tax break. It is actually a regressive tax that will widen the gap.

Becoming a Wealthy American

Americans say, on average, that it takes a net worth of $2.27 million to be considered "wealthy," according to a 2019 survey from Charles Schwab. Net worth means assets minus liabilities, so this is a picture of your total savings, including the value of your home, 401(k), and any other assets you may have, minus any debt.

How does that compare to the net worth of the typical American family?

The average net worth of all US families is $692,100, according to The Federal Reserve's Survey of Consumer Finances. If you look at the median, or those at the 50th percentile, the amount is significantly lower: $97,300 (and that may be a better gauge, since the super-rich can pull up the average).

According to the authors of *The One-minute Millionaire: The Enlightened Way of Wealth*, there are four paths to create wealth:

- Private business ownership
- Through the Internet
- Real Estate
- Equity investments through the stock market

Today, more than 95% of American companies and small businesses are owned by individuals. To the extent that these business owners are able to increase the market value of their companies, their personal net worth would increase exponentially. Studies show that 77% of wealth in the United States was made from owning a private company or professional firm.

People become entrepreneurs for different reasons. Some entrepreneurs are consumed by a business idea they simply must see become a reality, while others would rather work for themselves instead of someone else. An increasing number of Americans are entrepreneurs not out of choice but out of necessity. However, when one comes to be an entrepreneur, their success ultimately depends on operating a profitable business.

When you consider the decision to become an employee versus an entrepreneur or business owner, consider the four main reasons that your likelihood of becoming wealthy substantially decreases.

1. You become too comfortable to take risks

So, you have a job, which means you have income, meaning you can pay your bills. It's comfortable. You feel like you don't need to change anything, so you probably won't. It is important to push yourself to make a change in your comfortable lifestyle. If for some reason you lost your job, you would have no choice but to try to kick-start your dream in order to have a job or income. So, do something to shake up your life and see how just one change can push you to take charge and begin to change everything.

When you're working for someone else, you are building someone else's assets. This is well and good if you believe in their cause and just want to get by in life, but if you want to get rich, you're only hurting yourself. You're spending at least forty hours a week focusing on someone else. What about you, and what you want to do? Imagine if you had 40 free hours to work on something for yourself. It's a lot of time, right? Once you get out of your comfortable career rut, you'd have those 40 hours to dedicate to yourself and your own assets. Everything you put into yourself and your business will come right back to you. The money that you spend in the business can be deducted from your taxes and any income that is generated is yours alone!

2. Time is more valuable than money

Money is something you can save and something you can get more of if you know how. But time is fleeting. You'll never be able to make up time that you have already spent. And, as we just mentioned, when you spend time working for someone else, you're not able to use that time for yourself. Sure, you're making money while you work, but what if you finish your duties before lunch? You're wasting the other hours of the day doing nothing just to get that paycheck. Or, if you're on salary, you might be working way more than 40 hours, and not getting paid what you're worth. The company you work for is in charge of your time. They dictate your schedule, they tell you when you can leave early or have to stay late, and they tell you if you can take vacation time. When you work for yourself, you might work harder, but you're working for yourself and in charge of your own time.

3. You grow too focused on saving for a rainy day

Although saving money is smart (and we all know it makes very good sense), saving money does not help you to make money. Skipping Starbucks and making your coffee at home might save you five bucks, but it doesn't help you to earn any money. More than likely you are on a fixed income and just putting money aside. What you should be doing is investing in a business venture or at least growing your money in the stock market.

As you know, it's hard to get something started, but you have to come out of your comfort zone and take a chance! More than likely, it won't take off immediately, but this does not mean you are a failure. Sometimes, you have to be patient and let your business idea find its footing as you follow through on the things that will make it grow.

Don't expect everything to happen all at once, and don't get discouraged because over time you can achieve it!

CHAPTER 6

The Benefits of Entrepreneurship

No book about money would be complete without a chapter on business ownership. There are many benefits to owning and operating a business. Although the potential benefits more than outweigh the possible disadvantages and risks, it is important to get a complete understanding of what to expect if you decide to start a business. Let us keep in mind the slogan, "No risk, no return on investment."

We will begin with the downside of owning and operating a small business.

Time Commitment

When someone opens a small business, it's likely, at least in the beginning, that they will have few employees. This leaves all of the duties and responsibilities to the owner. Small-business owners report working more than eighty hours a week handling everything from purchasing to banking to advertising. This time commitment can place a strain on family and friends and add to the stress of launching a new business venture.

Risk

Even if the business has been structured to minimize the risk and liability to the owner, risk can't be completely eliminated. For instance, if an individual leaves a secure job to follow an entrepreneurial dream and the business fails, this financial setback can be hard to overcome. Beyond financial risk, entrepreneurs need to consider the risk from product liability, employee disagreements, and regulatory requirements

Uncertainty

Even though the business may be successful at the start, external factors such as downturns in the economy, new competitors entering the marketplace, or shifts in consumer demand may stall businesses growth. Even entrepreneurs who go through a comprehensive planning process will never be able to anticipate all potential changes in the business environment.

Financial Commitment

Even the smallest of business ventures requires a certain amount of capital to start. For many people starting small businesses, their initial source of funding is personal savings, investments, or retirement funds. Committing these types of funds to a business venture makes them unavailable for personal or family needs. In most cases where a small business receives start-up funding through a loan, the entrepreneur must secure the loan by pledging personal assets, such as a home. Risking the equity in one's home is a financial commitment not all entrepreneurs are willing to make.

Why Businesses Fail

In addition to looking at the disadvantages of owning a business, let us also analyze the reasons why most small businesses fail.

Lack of Planning

Starting a business without planning where you want to go is like starting a road trip with no final destination or a map to get there; you're bound to get lost. To avoid this mistake, set a clear goal of where you want to be and how you plan to get there.

Failure to Delegate

Within every business, someone needs to focus on the bigger picture and have an overview of everything happening internally and externally around the company. That person should be you, but not if your head is buried in the accounts. So, delegate and outsource all the tasks that can be done by others, and free yourself to concentrate on the bigger picture.

Unwillingness to Change

As a small business you can't afford to stand still while your market and the world around you moves forward. Adapt and develop your small business to be forward-thinking and innovative, not behind the times.

Forgetting That Cash Is King

A small business needs to monitor its cash flow closely. As soon as it loses track of the money, it's vulnerable to failure. Plot and analyze your income and expenditures to make sure your small business stays on the right financial track. Don't expect massive profits from the outset, but don't accept a loss, either.

Lack of Objective Targets

Failing to measure the success of campaigns, products, or services can be disastrous for a small business. Is that PR campaign you're running really worth the money? Does Twitter really bring traffic to your Web site? Know what to measure, and you'll know how successful you are.

Failure to Ask the Right Questions

When you're a small-business start-up, knowing which questions (and whom) to ask is difficult. There are numerous resources such as the SBA, local economic development agencies, and chambers of commerce that are great places to start. Part of the process is knowing what you don't know, and such organizations can help you figure that out.

How Businesses Succeed

Now that we have taken a brief look at the disadvantages and reasons why most businesses fail, let us look at the advantages.

Independence

Entrepreneurs are their own bosses. They make the decisions. They choose whom to do business with and what work they will do. They decide what hours to work, as well as what to pay and whether to take vacations. For many entrepreneurs, the freedom to control their destiny is enough to outweigh the potential risks.

Financial gain

Entrepreneurship offers a greater possibility of achieving significant financial rewards than working for someone else. Owning your own business removes the income restraints that exist when you're someone else's employee. Many entrepreneurs are inspired by the mega-millionaire entrepreneurs we see today, such as Steve Jobs, Elon Musk, Jeff Bezos, and Mark Zuckerberg.

Control

Being an entrepreneur enables one to be involved in the total operation of the business, from concept to design to creation, from sales to business operations and customer response. This ability to be totally immersed in the business is very satisfying to entrepreneurs who are driven by passion and creativity and possess a vision of what they aim to achieve. This level of involvement allows the business owner to truly create something of their own.

Prestige

Some entrepreneurs are attracted to the idea of being the boss. There is status in being the person in charge. In addition, there is the prestige and pride of ownership. When someone asks, "Who did this?" the entrepreneur can answer, "I did."

Equity

Entrepreneurship gives an individual the opportunity to build equity, which can be kept, sold, or passed on to the next generation. It's not uncommon for entrepreneurs to own multiple businesses throughout their life. They establish a company, run it for a while, and later sell it to someone else. The income from this sale can then be used to finance the next venture. If they're not interested in selling the business, the goal may be to build something that can be passed down to their children to help ensure their financial future. One thing is sure: in order to fully reap the financial benefits of a business venture, you need to be the owner.

Opportunity

Entrepreneurship creates an opportunity for a person to make a contribution. Most new entrepreneurs help the local economy. Through their innovations, a few contribute to society as a whole.

The entrepreneur's challenge is to balance decisiveness with caution—to be a person capable of seizing an opportunity but also one who has done enough preparatory work to be well informed and not assume unnecessary risk. Preparatory work includes evaluating the market opportunity, developing the product or service, preparing a good business plan, determining how much capital is needed, and making arrangements to obtain that capital.

Economists have analyzed a range of entrepreneurial successes and failures and identified key issues for up-and-coming business owners to carefully consider ahead of time. Taking these issues into account can reduce risk; ignoring them can contribute to failure. If you're considering entrepreneurship, ask yourself the following questions to make sure you're thinking about key business decisions.

Motivation

What is your incentive for starting a business? Is it money alone? Are you prepared to spend the time and money needed to get your business started? True, many entrepreneurs acquire great wealth. However, money is almost always tight in the early phases of a new business. Many entrepreneurs don't even take a salary until they can do so and still leave the firm with a positive cash flow.

Strategy

What products or services will your business provide? What differentiates your business idea and the products or services you will provide from others in the market? Who is your ideal customer? Who is your competition? Is the plan to compete solely on the basis of selling price? Price is important, but most economists agree that it's extremely risky to compete on price alone. Large firms that produce huge quantities have the advantage in lowering costs. It's also important to decide how you plan to manage and advertise your business.

Realistic vision

What kind of business do you want, and how much will it cost to get started? Will you need a loan? Is there a realistic vision of the enterprise's potential? How long will it take to make your product or service available? How long until you start making a profit? Insufficient operating funds are the cause of many business failures. Entrepreneurs often underestimate start-up costs and overestimate sales revenues in their business plans. Some analysts advise adding 50% to final cost estimates and reducing sales projections. Only then can the entrepreneur examine cash-flow projections and decide if he or she is ready to launch a new business.

Now let us take a look at the actual number of business owners and entrepreneurs in the United States. According to a recent report, around 534,000 new businesses start each month. Listed below are some important facts and statistics you should know if you are considering starting a small business:

- 82% of businesses that fail do so because of cash flow problems
- 50% of all small businesses are operated from home
- 84% of small business owners indicate that they're feeling optimistic about the future of their company
- 64% of small business owners begin with only $10,000 in capital
- Almost 25% of all small businesses begin with no financing
- Only 40% of all small businesses are profitable
- Only 64% of small businesses have a company website

A 2018 report by the U.S. Office of Advocacy revealed that small businesses employed 58.9 million people or 47.9% of the private workforce in 2015. Firms with fewer than 100 employees have the largest share of small business employment.

The Covid-19 Crisis of 2020

There is no way we can complete this chapter on entrepreneurship without addressing the current economic crisis shared by both large and small businesses in America and around the world. When I speak of the current economic climate, I refer specifically to the coronavirus pandemic of 2020. Although there is no research data available at this time, we are definitely in the midst of one of the worst economic crises of the century.

I will attempt to leave a brief synopsis of the situation for you the reader and for future generations to come. If there was ever an example of the need for individuals and business owners to have a long-term cash reserve for possible disasters, this is it. The impact of the crisis has hit every business across the board with very few exceptions. For barbershops, beauty salons, daycare centers, churches, restaurants, clubs, bars, and any business deemed "non-essential," the fallout has been horrendous.

In the beginning of 2020, the world found itself confronted with Covid-19, a strain of coronavirus that is airborne and can be easily transferred from human to human. The World Health Organization (WHO) declared that citizens in more than 250 countries around the world should refrain from direct contact both socially and on the job, avoid public transportation, and refrain from holding or attending large gatherings. Every citizen was encouraged to wear a face mask and gloves, and in some places it became mandatory. These measures were put into place in hopes of subduing an outbreak. Unfortunately, Covid-19 became a global pandemic.

The economic impact of this disaster is not yet recorded in numbers but can be viewed on three different levels.

The first level of impact is to those businesses and industries that bear the brunt of the damage. Stores, shops, and restaurants were forced to close to avoid face-to-face contact between customers.

The second level of impact is to manufacturers and businesses that support the first group. As fewer orders for products and an inability to operate due to the status of "non-essential" workers and employees refusing to report to work grow, so will the impact. Banks and lending institutions will be forced to absorb many loan defaults as a large portion of their customers cannot afford to stay in business as a result of more than two months with no ability to operate and no end to the pandemic in sight.

The Small Business Administration lists approximately 30 million small businesses across the United States. Collectively they employ almost 59 million people. By the end of June, up to half of them might be gone.

The third level of impact is a decrease in spending among individuals and families, even those with the designation of "essential workers" and stable jobs, due to fear of a huge financial aftershock.

As states take stronger and broader measures to contain the coronavirus, economist warn that time is running out to save America's small business community.

Across the country, state governments have taken actions to legally enforce "social distancing" in order to slow the spread of the coronavirus pandemic. This has ranged from Michigan's "Stay Home, Stay Safe" executive order to New York's economic "pause" and Massachusetts' 30-day closure of all dine-in bars and restaurants.

While lawyers question the legality of these measures, especially coercive actions like Michigan's, they have drawn little protest from the public at large. Yet many, if not most, small businesses say they don't have the resources to survive this kind of quarantine. State governments have moved quickly, shutting down their business communities in a matter of weeks. Yet the government has not moved equally quickly to protect those shops, service providers, and restaurants.

At the time of this writing, neither state nor federal governments have issued any significant relief to help businesses survive the ongoing quarantine, nor passed any major laws suspending debt and other obligations.

Instead, business owners are burning through their savings in order to survive, often reaching into their personal pockets to keep up with payments. That won't last long though. While some have already begun to close, analysts say that without a major rescue effort the small business community should expect a wave of permanent closures in the very near future.

CHAPTER 7

The Struggle is Real

When we discuss what it means to be chasing the dollar in America, one of our signature slogans comes to mind: "The struggle is real!"

As we take a deep look into the how people cope with the fear and reality of less than enough money to feed and clothe their families, we are reminded of two Negro spirituals that have reverberated in the chambers of the church in recent decades.

I won't complain by Reverend Paul Jones: "I've had some good days, I've had some hills to climb, I've had some weary days, why so much pain, but when I look around, and I think things over, all of my good days, they outweigh my bad days, so I won't complain."

Work it out! By Diane Williams: "All your money spent, how you going to pay your rent? Baby needs a pair of shoes, even got a light bill due. The telephone disconnect, waiting on your next paycheck…"

These are just short excerpts of song lyrics which breed hope and faith that a better day will come when "the struggle is real."

In this chapter we will take a close look at many of the behaviors and business practices of those who struggle to obtain the dollar and a profit, in some cases at the expense of financially illiterate consumers.

Chasing the Dollar in America

We will first address the topics of earning money on the black market and of deviant behavior as they pertain to making money. I will even share a few examples from my own life and professional career as an accountant and businessman. While attending classes at Drexel University, I took an elective course of particular interest called "The Psychology of Deviant Behavior." (I am very proud to say that I received an A grade in this class at the end of the semester). I was very interested in this curriculum because I wanted to better understand why some people leave the norms of society and engage in deviant behavior which is usually unacceptable to the majority of citizens.

In this class, I learned that there was a group of individuals who think *outside the box*. These individuals are known as *outliers*. They deviate from the norms of society. They exist outside what is called the bell curve which establishes the normal distribution of behavior in society. It is a personality trait shared by many individuals throughout history and in every aspect of society. Usually, there is some sort of event or life experience that causes an individual to become deviant and move away from the norms of society.

Whether it's prostitution (which is one of the oldest deviant businesses in the world), street gambling, dealing illegal drugs, or simply selling your food stamps for cash, just to name a few, "the struggle is real," especially amongst the poorest and least–educated population.

The individuals in this group have decided that the system is not fair and is stacked against them. They believe that they can beat the system by engaging in acts of deviant behavior as it relates to obtaining money. In many cases, it's all about survival for people who are unprepared to meet the challenges of daily life.

Let me take a minute to say that in no way am I condoning or justifying these types of behavior. However, I think it is very important to acknowledge and address their existence.

Throughout my professional life experience, I have discovered they there are many acts of deviant behavior relating to obtaining money and improving personal finances.

One of the areas that I am very familiar with is the filing of false and misleading income tax returns. I found through experience that it is not uncommon for individuals of all income levels to lie and cheat on their annual income tax returns. I experienced this personally in my own income tax practice. One of the most common acts of fraud was the adding of false dependents on a tax return to increase the refund, especially those relating to the *unearned income credit.*

Another act that I found very common on income tax returns was the reporting of donations and contributions to churches and non-profit organizations that never took place. You see, it's all about the penalty verses the reward. Smart deviant individuals know that the worst that will happen if caught is that the Internal Revenue Service will recalculate the return and increase the tax liability, thereby reducing the expected refund. It's a numbers game. If you know how the Internal Revenue Service internal audit controls operate, you understand that they analyze the tax returns on a comparison basis, looking for the outliers. If you stay below that threshold you will probably never get caught.

One more example of deviant behavior relating to tax evasion that I experienced was clergy or ministers who don't report their income from offerings, and in some cases, business revenue. One minister who was a personal friend of mine was operating a business in the church name and depositing the revenues into his personal bank account. He failed to take into account that the IRS can audit you at any time and ask you to verify the sources of your income. If you have cash or real estate that you obtained or purchased, this could trigger the IRS to ask for proof you reported all of your income. In his case, the IRS seized his bank accounts and calculated his unreported income based on all the assets that he obtained over several years. This process wiped his finances out completely.

While engaged in my profession as a tax preparer and bookkeeper, I witnessed many businesspeople who cheated on their sales and usage tax returns. It was not uncommon for business owners to underreport sales revenue to minimize sales tax owed to state governments which collect sales tax through the sale of goods and services.

I have witnessed many commercial and retail business owners who tell you, "if you pay cash, I won't charge you taxes!" So you see, it's "all about the dollar," and the struggle and hustle are very real and alive in all aspects of today's society.

Please let me take this moment to say that my purpose is not to change society or redeem those who engage on a daily basis in acts of deviant behavior in order to generate money and capital, but I do have a message for the individuals in this group. My message is simply this: "If you engage in deviant behaviors that are considered fraudulent or operate on the black market, you might want to consider saving and investing a portion of your income before you get caught and possibly end up in jail or prison."

Let's be very honest. "It's a numbers game," I always tell people. As an accountant and financial advisor, I'm deep into numbers and statistics on a daily basis. If you do the research, you can predict the probability of getting caught in the act of deviant behavior that you are engaged in.

Let me get personal and confess that I am not without sin when it comes to engaging in deviant behavior in my own profession. One of my most lucrative hustles was accepting payments (usually around $200) from mortgage brokers who requested the preparation of false paycheck stubs and tax returns needed to secure mortgage loans for various clients. It was easy, quick money, and generated a nice cash flow for 15 or 20 minutes of work!

Another act of deviant behavior that I engaged in was the preparation of fraudulent tax returns. The tax return business is a hustle, and most individuals are looking for the preparer who can get them the best refund. In reality, there is no crystal ball or opportunity to increase a refund except for knowing the tax law, every credit, and every write-off that an individual is entitled too. My most famous hustle was adding a schedule C–business income profit and loss form–to the tax return and reporting a loss from business income. By creating a fake business and reporting a loss from business operations, the loss reduces the tax liability generated from wages and thereby increases the individuals refund by reducing the total tax liability. When you are chasing the dollar, you often do whatever you can to beat the competition and gain a reputation for outperforming the rest.

Most individuals who engage in deviant business practices are actually very intelligent. In many cases, they know the system and the penalties they face if caught in the act. Many drug dealers know the penalty for being caught selling drugs. They know how much time they will serve based on the quantity of drugs that they were moving when they got caught. To minimize their risk, many drug dealers move their drugs in small amounts.

Some of the smarter drug dealers have been known to set aside a reserve fund for legal services if they get caught. It is not uncommon for them to put aside $5,000 or even $10,000 to pay an attorney to represent them.

Most women engaged in prostitution know the laws and their rights regarding this practice. The first question that they will ask you is, "Are you a police or law enforcement officer?" Most prostitutes are very familiar with the laws as they relate to *entrapment*. Most already know the penalties for first time offenders. "It's all about the dollar…and the struggle is real!"

Let us take a look at some of the ways people steal money to survive.

Identity Theft

We begin with what is known as *identity theft*.

According to recent research, in 2016 identity theft cost consumers more than $16 billion. Some 15.4 million consumers were victims of identity theft or fraud last year, according to a new report from Javelin Strategy & Research. That's up 16 percent from 2015, and the highest figure recorded since the firm began tracking fraud instances in 2004.

"All of the underlying types of fraud we measure are up," says Al Pascual, a senior vice president and research director for Javelin.

Card-not-present fraud—transactions made online or via phone where the cardholder does not need to present the physical card to complete the purchase—jumped the most, increasing 40 percent compared to 2015. Account takeover fraud—where thieves used stolen login information to access a consumer's accounts—rose 31 percent, and instances where fraudsters opened new accounts in a consumer's name were up 20 percent. In all, thieves stole $16 billion, the report found, nearly $1 billion more than in 2015.

Our password "hygiene" is very poor, and criminals know it. You should create unique, complex passwords for each of your accounts, and enable two-factor authentication where you can, Pascual advises. Thieves often test lists of passwords stolen in one breach against other accounts to see, for example, if your old Yahoo password is still the one you use for your checking account.

Using a virtual debit or credit card number from issuers including Citi, Bank of America, or start-up Privacy.com, can help cut off thieves from accessing your accounts. Cards can be set up for only a single transaction, or usable for only a single site, rending a stolen card number useless. Another tactic to consider: Placing a credit freeze with Experian, Equifax, and TransUnion. This drastic measure prevents anyone, including you, from opening new lines of credit in your name.

Shoplifting

While most shoplifters are amateurs, there are growing numbers of organized theft rings and people who make their living by stealing from retail stores. Amateur shoplifters can be highly skilled, and some steal almost every day but don't do it to make a living. Most amateurs are opportunistic, crude in their methods, and are frequently detected. Professional shoplifters run the gamut from being highly skilled to thug-like. Some professionals work in teams or use elaborate distraction scenarios. The crude professionals sometimes use force and fear much like gang intimidation and often commit grab-and-run thefts. Being a professional means that they steal merchandise for a living, and like other trades, practice makes perfect. Thoughtful professionals are very difficult to stop in a society where retail stores openly display their merchandise.

Shoplifters come in all shapes, sizes, ages, and sexes, and vary in ethnic background, education, and economic status. Some shoplifters steal for the excitement, some steal out of desire, some steal for need, some steal out of peer pressure, and some steal because for them it is simply a business transaction. Some shoplifters are compulsive, some opportunistic, and some are mentally ill and don't know any better. Some shoplifters are desperate from drug addiction, alcoholism, or living on the street. Children and elderly persons sometimes steal without realizing they are committing a crime. Most shoplifters try to rationalize their crime by thinking the large retailer can afford the loss.

In urban cities, it is not unusual to find a network of fences that send out teams of shoplifters into retail stores to shoplift specific items, much like filling an order for a customer. These fences only pay 10-20 cents on the dollar to the thieves, but sometimes pay their room, board, and provide training on how to steal and defeat anti-theft technology. Some fences have been known to bail their workers out of jail when caught or provide for their legal defense. This creates a kind of strange street loyalty much like the tale of Oliver Twist.

The Real Cost of Retail Theft

Theft from stores, including employee and vendor theft, costs retailers many billions of dollars per year. Shoplifting losses vary by store type but can account for about one-third of the total inventory shrinkage. It is estimated that shoplifting occurs 330-440 million times per year at a loss of $10-$13 billion dollars. Nationwide, that equates to 1.0-1.2 million shoplift incidents every day at a loss rate of $19,000-$25,300 dollars stolen per minute. When you factor in employee and vendor theft, this sum skyrockets to an estimate of over $33 billion dollars stolen per year. Whole retail store chains have gone out of business due to their inability to control theft. And worse yet, these losses are passed on to us, the consumer.

Panhandling

Although this form of generating income is not necessarily deviant, we will include it here because the struggle is real. Let us look at the people who are at the very bottom, who must resort to the worst methods of generating income in order to feed themselves on a daily basis. Let us turn our attention to the art of *panhandling*, a fancy word for begging.

When you see a panhandler out on the street, what is the first thing that comes to mind? Many see panhandlers as lazy people, alcoholics perhaps, and definitely freeloaders. What if everything that society thought about panhandlers happened to be wrong?

In a recent survey, 94% of panhandlers use the funds that they get from the donations of others to simply purchase the food they need. Some panhandlers do have the ability to make upwards of $80,000 per year, but those are the exception rather than the rule. In San Francisco, for example, the average daily intake for a panhandler is just $25 per day, and some people have been living this way for five years or more. Many must opt for the cheapest food options available, which means high fat and low nutritional content.

Who is The Typical Panhandler?

Three Fast Facts About Panhandling:

- Only 3% of panhandlers don't want some form of permanent housing that would help to get them off of the street.
- 48% of panhandlers are African American.
- One out of every four panhandlers in the United States has served in the military at some point in time.

Drug use can be problematic in panhandlers. Forty-four percent of panhandlers admit using part of their daily take on drugs or alcohol at least once per week. One in four panhandlers meet the clinical definition of being an alcoholic, and another 32% are addicted to at least one drug other than alcohol.

Eighty-two percent of panhandlers are homeless. The average panhandler asks people for assistance for about 6 hours per day. The average panhandler also asks for help every day of the week. This is practically a full-time job. The average person on the street who is asking for assistance has been panhandling for 4.6 years. Fifty-eight percent have been panhandling for at least five years. Some panhandlers look for other forms of secondary income as assistance. This may include plasma donations, selling drugs, or collecting food stamps.

Most panhandlers are men, and the percentage can exceed 80% in many communities. Up to 80% of panhandlers have spent time in jail and more than 20% have spent at least one stint in a state prison. Most crimes that are committed by panhandlers are poverty related, with most being accused of trespassing or theft.

Fifty percent of panhandlers in a 1993 survey stated that they had been mugged within the last 12 months at least once. Thirty-six of the 50 largest cities in the United States have made public begging a criminal offense.

Up to 80% of panhandlers choose to sleep outside full time so they can have a cash reserve for food if they don't get help during the day. Single city surveys show that up to 40% of the homeless population may engage in panhandling activities at least one day per week. Panhandling is more likely to occur in urban than suburban areas, while business centers are the most targeted place. At the same time, business owners are the most likely demographic to contact the police when panhandlers are outside of a business. In large metropolitan areas, it is believed that over $4 million per year could be going to charities that provide social services instead of panhandlers.

Outside of the US, the children of a family will commonly beg in order to support themselves and their families.

Our takeaway is that panhandlers may be difficult to take seriously when you see them out on the street drinking a 40 and asking for spare change. That image, however, is not always reflective of what people do. There's no denying that living on the streets is a difficult experience. If it is fine for someone to have a couple drinks after a hard day at work, why isn't it fine for someone to have a couple drinks after a hard day of life?

The problem is that an uncaring attitude toward all panhandlers because of the actions of a few creates future problems that will ultimately create even more panhandlers. When more than 60% of panhandlers make less than $25 per day, and when more than 60% of them are disabled in some way, that is not a life that anyone would wish on their greatest enemy. Yet there is an expectation that panhandlers can and should crawl up out of the mess unassisted and contribute to society just because a few people take advantage of others.

Does a dollar here and a dollar there help? Maybe… or maybe not. No one can really know. The point is that whatever someone can do to help within their own power they should do. That's part of the human experience—lending a helping hand up when they can and knowing that there will be a helping hand available when it is needed.

Scams!

When it comes to deviant behavior and making money, scams are everywhere! No matter if you live in a small town or large city, you are not exempt from scam artists.

Whether it is making a phone call to a senior citizen telling them that they are in collections in order to pressure them to make a payment on a bill that doesn't exist, or posing as a social security administrator updating their records in order to get their personal information, the scams against seniors are endless. They are a primary target for scammers.

Some scammers are consumers themselves. Chargeback fraud, also known as *friendly fraud*, occurs when a consumer makes an online shopping purchase with their credit card, and then request a chargeback from the issuing bank after receiving the purchased goods or services. Once approved, the chargeback cancels the financial transaction, and the consumer receives a refund of the money they spent.

Another fraud that takes advantage of the system involves food stamps. Under the federal guidelines for the proper use of food stamps, now known as electronic benefits transfer or EBT, the funds which are placed on the EBT card can only be used to purchase food. The funds can never be used as cash purchase for non-food items nor in most cases "prepared food." However, there is a glitch in the system that allows a recipient to get cash even though it is not permitted. The recipient goes to a store that has a return policy and purchases food and related items. After about 10 minutes, they return to the store and request a refund. If the recipient is friendly with the cashier or have a friend or family member working at the store, the person processing the refund of the goods can actually refund cash. This is how you turn funds allocated for food only into cash to be used for virtually any purchase.

As consumers become more and more conscientious about their spending during the recent pandemic, experts expect that friendly fraud will become a more common issue and practice. Prior to the pandemic, a 2014 VISA report estimated losses from friendly fraud to be $11.8 billion. The current level of losses due to friendly fraud during the pandemic is not yet available but experts expect the total to exceed recent statistics.

In a surreal combination of two different deviant behaviors, I have heard many stories regarding scams in the prostitution business from close friends. There are three scams that are most common.

- Asking for a deposit for services by using phone apps like Cash App, Venmo, or PayPal, and never showing up for service.
- Asking for gas money to get to the client location and never showing up for service.
- Telling the client that the provider does not accept cash and requires a gift card for services. After the client picks up a gift card, the provider asks the client to take a picture of both sides of the gift card for verification. After receiving a picture of the gift card, the provider has all the information needed to use the funds on the card.

At this time, I would like to share with you another money scam that I witnessed personally. While working as a cashier at a drug store chain, I witnessed a customer coming into the store to purchase a reloadable debit card. He looked for the youngest cashier who would likely be inexperienced with recognizing counterfeit money. He handed the young cashier (still in high school) $700 in counterfeit twenty-dollar bills. The young cashier accepted the money and processed the transaction.

Unfortunately, the counterfeit money was not discovered by the manager until after the end of the shift. In order to cancel the card, the store manager would have had to cancel the transaction within one hour. By the time the discovery took place, it was too late, leaving the store cheated out of $700.

Another personal money scam that I experienced involves people who pretend to want a relationship over the internet. These people are skilled at soliciting money from people like myself who are emotionally gullible. This happens when you seek personal relationships in the wrong places, especially without meeting in person. They may claim they have no money to travel but would love to meet you and spend time with you, and in some cases, promise to marry you. Most of the time, they send beautiful pictures and even intimate pictures to pique your emotions, but you never know who the person really is. Nearly every time, it's a scammer. This scam happens across the country and even more so internationally.

My story involves an international scam. A person posing as a beautiful woman engaged with me on Facebook Messenger and started an internet relationship. This person then asked to move the conversation to another messaging app called WhatsApp. After six months of beautifully stimulating daily conversations, the so-called woman asked me to send her money to travel from Ghana, Africa to the US. Foolishly, I wired her the amount of money she requested via Western Union, even though Western Union warned me to never send money to anyone you have never met in person. In fact, you must sign a disclosure assuring Western Union that you have met this person, or they will not process the transaction. After I sent the money for airplane travel, food, and lodging, I never heard from this person again. Later I learned that the pictures I received were those of an Instagram model.

A similar experience happened to me on a local basis right here in the US. I met a beautiful lady on WhatsApp. We were in a relationship for nine months when she finally asked me to send her money to come visit me. In this case, she was supposedly in the military. She sent me many pictures of her in her military uniform, as well as many seductive pictures. We also used video chat, so I was sure she was real because I saw her face. Her scam story was that while on active duty, she had no access to her money. She sent me a copy of her bank statement, which showed plenty of money in the account, and so I believed her.

Once again, I sent a woman money to travel along with an additional $500 (the fee that she claims she had to pay to get an official leave request). Once again, she took my money and never came to visit; but in this case, she continued to stay in communication, making excuses and trying to get more money. In the end, I blocked her from contacting me.

When you hear about some money scams, you can't believe that anyone would fall for them, they seem so obvious! But there is a good reason for that. Money scammers don't want to work hard; they want to pick only the low hanging fruit. If a scam is evident to you, you're not going to fall for it. The scammers would waste time trying to hook you.

But not everyone is quite so savvy. If someone falls for the first step of what seems like an obvious scam to most people, the scammers can proceed because the victim has proven themselves an easy mark. There are even lists available for sale on the dark web of people who are easy prey for money scams. Things like the old Nigerian prince scam are still happening because they work on a small number of people. But a small number of victims is all a scammer needs.

But our readers are unlikely to fall for what are clearly scams, so we're going to make you aware of some more subtle ones. Listed below are some of the top ten money scams.

1. Skimmer Scammers

If you were to lose your wallet or have it stolen, you would know it right away; and could cancel all of your credit and debit cards before too much or any damage was done. But if you're the victim of a card skimmer, you probably won't know it until it's too late.

A card skimmer is a tiny device that is hidden in places like ATMs and gas pumps. They're hard to spot; just a bit of plastic over a regular card swiping slot, but there is a reader inside that records the information on your card when you swipe it. Some of these scammers also install small cameras near the keypads so they can record your PIN.

To help avoid this money scam, only use ATMs inside your bank. The doors are locked at night, and there are likely cameras around, which makes these ATMs a much less attractive target than the ones in places like bars and convenience stores. When you enter your PIN, cover the keypad with your hand to block any camera that might be watching.

2. Work from Home Scams

Every person's dream is working from home on an everyday basis. After all, it's a dream to avoid the stresses of commuting back-and-forth from our homes to the workplace. Offers to earn a lot of money for very little labor sound too good to be true, and they are. But there are plenty of legitimate ways to make money working from home, so it can be hard to separate the scams from the legitimate opportunities.

Any job promising pay that seems too good to be true is. You can make extra money working from home, and there are some jobs that even offer full-time employment with benefits. But no work from home opportunity is going to make you rich overnight. You shouldn't have to pay for anything to work from home. No legitimate job asks for money from employees. Would you pay to go to work at a brick and mortar job? No, you wouldn't. A work from home job should be seen no differently.

3. MLM Schemes

If you have a Facebook account, you probably have at least one friend raving about the benefits of some kind of patch or drink that has helped them lose weight or feel more energetic. These are multi-level marketing schemes; they used to be known as pyramid schemes.

The people involved in these scams post glossy photos of their "free" trips to low rent tourist destinations for "sales conferences" and of the brand-new luxury car they were awarded for meeting some sales goal. The sellers are encouraged to buy boxes and boxes of whatever miracle product is being peddled and then to annoy everyone they come into contact with into buying some of it, or better yet, selling it themselves.

While money can be made from these money scams, it's only the people at the very top who manage to do it. What happens to everyone else is that they end up with a garage full of product they've bought and paid for but can't sell. These things have ruined marriages, friendships, and family relationships. Stay away!

4. The Chinese Consulate Scam

This scam is perpetrated by robocalls. If you live in an area that has a significant Chinese population, you might get calls from someone speaking Mandarin telling you they're from the Chinese consulate and you're being investigated for some kind of financial crime in China. If the person on the other end of the line takes the initial bait, they're transferred to a live person who instructs them that if they wire money to a bank in Hong Kong, the case will be resolved.

I have been getting a ton of these calls. I live in New Orleans, which doesn't have a sizeable Chinese community. However, my cell phone number is still a New York City number, and that's why it's is on the scammer's call list. I don't speak Mandarin and never answer calls from unfamiliar numbers, but the caller left a voicemail. When I checked it and heard Mandarin, I did some research, and this is what turned up.

This goes for any phone related scam: if you don't recognize a number, don't answer it. If you do answer it, you've been marked as an active number. At best, you will end up getting dozens more scam-related calls. At worst, the person on the other end may actually get some kind of sensitive information out of you. Ignore these calls when they come in and block the number.

Another thing to point out is that if you've ever registered your phone number to the Do Not Call Registry, the registration never expires. Some people have been getting emails purporting to be from the FTC telling them they need to re-enroll their number. This is just a ploy to get people to provide their phone numbers for more scams like the fake Chinese consulate!

5.   Phishing Scams

Various types of phishing scams have been around for ages, but there is one that has become more prevalent lately. I've been getting these for a while; however, they always end up in my junk mail, so I know immediately that they're a scam. Phishing is an attempt to get personal information from you, like bank account information or passwords, by sending a seemingly legitimate request.

The one I've been getting lately is from iTunes, but it really isn't. It's an email with a fake invoice attached that shows I've recently purchased an app telling me I need to click on the included link because there is a problem with my payment, and I need to re-enter my payment information.

No one, not the IRS, your bank, or your credit card company is going to send you an email asking for your passwords or account numbers. Don't even open these emails if you're at all suspicious. Call whatever company is claiming to have sent the email and verify if they actually did. Or, just ignore it.

6. Jury Duty Scam

Getting a jury duty notice isn't my favorite piece of mail (I just got one last week), but I know it's part of being a good citizen to show up on the appointed day and keep my fingers crossed that I get dismissed early. I'm currently 3-0, so I'm hoping to continue my streak now that I'm in New Orleans!

I've never just ignored a jury duty notice, but if you have, you might get nervous when a U.S. Marshal gives you a ring and threatens to arrest or fine you for skipping out. The fake marshal may even give the name and badge number of a real marshal and ask you to wire money to pay the fine or buy a pre-paid debit or gift card and use it to pay the fine. Once you buy the card and give the caller the code, they can spend it. Now, I think most of us are unlikely to fall for the gift card version of this scam, but the money wiring version might be more convincing. And go to jury duty the next time you get a notice!

7. Student Loan Scam

Tens of millions of us have student loan debt, so it's an area ripe for scammers. The scammers claim to be with the government or one of the well-known student loan servicing companies like Nelnet or Great Lakes. They offer to reduce or even eliminate your student loan debt through programs you're pre-approved for. It can cost hundreds of dollars to enroll, and you'll be asked to pay the entire fee up front. Once you pay the fee, guess what happens next? That's right, nothing. The scammer has your money and disappears into the night.

If you're struggling with your student loan debt, you may be eligible for a legitimate program, or you can look into refinancing through Lend Key, another legitimate option.

8. Debt Collection Scams

If you have past due debts, they may be sold to a third party. The third party tries to collect on the debt and gets to keep any money they recover. If you do have past due debt, it can be hard to tell a legitimate debt collector from a scammer.

You knew you owed money to Company Y, but the debt was sold to Company Z. On top of that, some legitimate debt collectors use rough, high-pressure tactics similar to scam debt collectors, making it harder to separate fact from fiction. You have the right to ask for proof of the debt under The Fair Debt Collection Practices Act. Doing so scares off most scammers immediately. You can also look at your credit report and see if the debt is listed, although keep in mind that past due accounts drop off your report after seven years, so even if it doesn't appear, it may be legitimate.

A real debt collector won't ask you for payment via a non-traceable method like a wire transfer. If the collector threatens you with prison if you don't pay the debt, that's another definite red flag. We don't have debtor's prisons (yet). This type of scam can go on for a long period of time, as the phone call harassment will continue until the victim breaks down and makes a payment over the phone. A few months later, the same vicious cycle begins once again to acquire more money from a helpless victim.

9. Online Shopping Scams

Nearly 80% of Americans shop online, which means there is a big pool of potential targets for scammers. The most common scam is ordering and paying for something that just never arrives. In other cases, you might receive an inferior product to the one you ordered or even an empty box!

Only buy from companies you've heard of. Yes, Suzy's House of Pillows might have pillows cheaper than Amazon, but you don't know Suzy! If you do choose to shop on an unfamiliar site, make sure the address starts with *https*. It's the *s* that's important. It means the site uses an extra layer of security called an SSL, a Secured Socket Layer. If you use Google Chrome as your browser, they have recently made it very easy to tell if a site uses encryption, which helps protect your data. On the far-left side of your address bar, you'll see a closed padlock on sites that do use encryption and a red triangle with an exclamation inside on sites which still don't.

Another way to protect yourself from online shopping scams is to use a credit card rather than a debit card to pay. If you don't receive anything or received something other than what you ordered, you can dispute the charge. The credit card company takes care of the rest. I've had to do this a few times, and the credit card company always found in my favor and refunded my money. Some debit cards offer this too, but when you pay with a credit card, it's the credit cards company's money, when you use a debit card, it's your money. These disputes can take a few days or weeks to resolve, and you may not be refunded your cash until it's settled.

10. Out and About Scams

Some money scams happen in person rather than over the internet or phone. But your money is still at risk. If you come to New Orleans, here is a classic to avoid: someone will walk up and say, "I bet you I can tell where you got them shoes." The correct answer is "On my feet." If you don't answer correctly, you owe the guesser $5.

Avoid anyone handing you anything, a CD, a bracelet, or a trinket of some kind. There are "monks' all over the High Line in New York City doing this one. They offer you a "blessing" while jamming some kind of cheap bracelet onto your wrist and then ask for a "donation."

This is another big city classic: you're walking in a crowded area, and someone bumps into you which causes them to drop a bag or a box. You hear glass tinkling. When you think back later, you'll realize it was the sound of already broken glass hitting the sidewalk, which sounds very different than an intact glass object shattering. But at the moment, you're flustered because the person who bumped you is yelling and making a scene, accusing you of having just broken whatever object is in the bag and demanding payment to buy a replacement.

The best way to avoid these kinds of scams is just to ignore the person and keep walking. Don't take anything being handed to you and if you do take it out of reflex, drop it and then walk away. Just like every other scammer, these people are looking for easy, compliant marks who are just going to hand over the cash to escape an awkward situation.

Listed below are the top 10 online scams in 2019.

1. Remote PC Repair Scams

This scam originates out of India. Victims are contacted by a phone call from scam artists claiming to be a representative of a high-tech computer firm. The call is a warning to the victim that their computer has been infected or could be under a threat of being infected by a vicious malware virus that will severely damage their internal operating system. The alleged "representative" encourages the victim to go on-line and allow them to troubleshoot the computer to fix all of the related issues immediately.

The representative will use this time to infect the computer with a real malware virus that does real harm, and then force the owner to go to a third-party website to confirm the damage. The goal of this scam is to force the computer owner to immediately pay for unnecessary repair work over the phone by using a credit card.

First, never give anyone remote access to your computer; you should hire a local repair service whenever possible. It's rare that a PC rep-resentative would call a computer user to alert them of a virus threat. Unfortunately, too many individuals have fallen for this scam and often report their personal identity has been stolen soon after the phone encounter.

Consumers who have been contacted by tech support scammers could have had their personal information breached. It is highly recom-mended that everyone targeted by scammers obtains identity theft protection service immediately. There are several companies offering identity theft protection in the US. I strongly recommend the protec-tion provided by Experian. You can get protected right now for FREE for 30 days with up to $1 Million in Identity Theft Insurance by visiting their website.

2. Fake/Counterfeit Scam

Today's internet world has brought a number of online stores to the forefront, as they cater to all needs. It's often too difficult to determine which sites are legitimate and which pose a threat to your personal information. Many of these unreliable online stores are known to origi-nate out of China, and mimic actual websites that sell name brands. The attraction is selling popular items (which are counterfeit) at a reduced price to a very willing clientele.

The goal is to get them to make impulse purchases, providing their personal information so it can be sold on the black market. In some cases, identity thieves will actually send their counterfeit products via the mail to unsuspecting victims to keep them clueless that their identity has been stolen.

Too often, large corporations are the first to discover these fake online stores and take immediate action to have them shut down. If you need to verify the authenticity of a website, then contact one of the brands that you're interested in purchasing from by using the information provided on their contact page.

3.   Fraudulent/Fake Check Scam

One of the more popular scams currently taking place is scam artists convincing unknowing victims to accept a fraudulent check in exchange for cash. They send out an elaborate email detailing how they're having difficulty cashing a check and would anyone be kind enough to help them gain immediate cash into their hands. Whoever responds to their request will receive an added bonus for their troubles. The endorsed check bounces and the victim is left with no money in their bank account. Consumers who have been contacted by fake check scammers could have had their personal information breached. It is highly recommended that everyone targeted by scammers obtains identity theft protection service immediately.

4.   Pets-for-Sale Scam

A pet-for-sale scam involves creating a fake website that offers pet adoption or provides individuals an opportunity to make a donation to a fictitious animal nursery. The website showcases a wide variety of animals that can be adopted at significantly lower than the market price. Victims are required to only pay for the insurance and other fees associated with shipping their new pet to their home. The only form of payment accepted is a MoneyGram, Western Union, or a money transfer to an overseas bank account. Of course, there is no pet.

Avoid paying for a pet by transferring money into another person's bank account. Scam Guard can assist with securing information of reliable animal breeders in your area.

5.   Grant Scam

This scheme involves scam artists purchasing legitimate consumer information from the top corporations in our country. These businesses are led to believe this inquiry is an opportunity to offer some form of financial assistance to customers who have severe debt issues.

These scam artists then pose as government officials offering a unique opportunity to receive grant money for a processing fee. The goal is to get victims to give up their immediate savings for an opportunity to gain that last big payday. Plus, after completing the scam, the personal information gained will be sold to the highest bidder on the black market.

6.   Collection Agency Scam

Scam artists are well aware that collection agencies have the right to contact individuals who are behind in their monthly bills. While it is not illegal to contact consumers via email, the FDCPA stipulates that debt collectors can use the mail or call debtors on the phone. Assume that legitimate collection agencies will adhere to these guidelines.

In this case scammers send emails presenting themselves as a representative of a fictitious collection agency threatening a lawsuit unless
the victim settles their current debt. Some scam artists support their
claims with factual information about the person's bad credit history.
Do not respond to these emails and check your credit report if you
do not recognize this supposed debt.

7. House/Vacation Property Rental Scam

The collapse of the housing market has made prospective owners opt
toward renting homes and vacation properties. Scam artists have used
this trend to attract new targets by advertising fictitious properties for
rent. They provide victims with attractive pictures and detailed information on the property.

The suggested rental price will be well below the current market, and
the scammer will only converse with prospective renters via a VOIP
phone number that's located in a foreign country. After an agreement is
in place, the first month's rental payment must be made through a money transfer process. Victims pay to stay at a property that doesn't exist.

8. Payday Loan Scam

Scam artists love preying on victims at their utmost vulnerable moment. Usually, during difficult financial times, victims resort to taking
out a high-interest loan.

Scam artists take advantage of this situation by creating a website that
entices desperate individuals to apply for a loan to clear the debt.
Representatives from these fake websites call victims to tell them they
have qualified for a low-interest loan, but to gain immediate access
to the money, the victim must pay a security fee. This payment is to
cover costs of verifying that the individual has the income necessary to

repay the loan. Other variations of this scam include requesting bank account information to set up a direct deposit of the loan money. In the end, the loan never follows through, as the victim is out of the fee payment and still in debt.

9. Timeshare Resale Scam

Timeshare property has been one of the biggest scams for decades, as the thought of sharing an ideal vacation resort property at a reduced cost is irresistible. The scam preys on the myth that the property can be unloaded for a large profit.

First, the timeshare owner must pay an upfront fee that includes an updated property appraisal, closing costs and broker's fee. To protect yourself, read the contract closely, because the wording can be confusing yet still binding if you put your signature on the dotted line.

10. Working from Home Scam

With more and more people looking for the opportunity to make some money on the side, work from home scams have become more prevalent. Scammers are moving from the classifieds and pennysavers to the internet.

This scam centers around setting up a fictitious website that offers a work-at-home position within the international shipping department. The victim goes through the interview process on instant messenger or email correspondence. Once hired, the company begins to send packages to the new employee's home with explicit instructions on how to inspect the product before shipping it elsewhere.

Soon after, communication between the company and employee ceases, as they receive a fictitious paycheck that's greater than time worked.

Once the employee is finally able to get in contact with their employer about the overpayment, the company confirms the mistake and tells the employee to send the back the difference before depositing the check. Unfortunately, the victim will receive notice that the paycheck has bounced with no recourse to recover the money from their employer, who has now vanished.

Corporate Greed and Immorality

Now that we have discussed earning money on the black market and through deviant behaviors, we will turn our attention to some of the recent business practices of corporate America that are unethical but, in many cases, create a competitive edge to those who engage in such practices.

Once again, I will begin the discussion with a personal experience that I encountered during the course of my professional accounting career. I was working as an accountant for a company that is well-known in the industry for controlling nearly 90% of government contracts for highway maintenance. It was regular policy for the company to bid on almost all government contracts related to the services they provided. In some instances, in order to outbid other competitors, it was necessary to underbid the contracts to a degree that there was actually no opportunity to earn a profit from the completion of the contract.

So, I am sure your next question is, "Why would a company outbid its competitors by 'low balling' its bid to a level below the profit margin of the contract?" The answer to the question is very simple: the company was determined to maintain control of the contracts by any means necessary.

But here is the piece of the bidding process that you need to focus on and understand. The company had mastered the process of bidding on a contract with no profit and yet was still making a profit off the contract. Let me explain to you exactly what they would do: The company would accept the contract at a rate and cost that was totally unprofitable and then turn around and subcontract it out to its competitors, taking a 7% management fee off the top. Another way of looking at it is they would subcontract it out to a competitor for 93% of the original bid.

By now I am sure your next question is why would a subcontracting competitor accept a contract with literally no opportunity to make a profit or even break even?

The answer to this question is also very simple but may surprise you. Most of the time, the companies who accept these kinds of contracts are small and just need an opportunity to keep their staff together until they can bid on a more lucrative contract with more profit. So, they have no choice but to accept the terms of the contract because their company is in "survival mode."

The manager in charge of contract negotiations explained to me that this is how our company makes money on a contract we bid on that actually had no opportunity to earn a profit. We just "farm it out" and take our management fee off the top, he explained. This is just one personal example of a conglomerate taking advantage of a smaller business.

Don't think that the poor and needy are the only ones involved in deviant behavior to obtain money. Deviant behavior happens across all walks of life. Many of the richest individuals in our country are guilty of fraud and tax evasion. It's seems like no one really wants to pay taxes. Many corporations and businesses have been fined by the IRS for filing false financial statements of earnings and false corporate tax returns.

In more recent years, no place has witnessed more deviant behavior than Wall Street. People like Bernie Madoff became infamous for stealing billions of dollars from investors. Prosecutors estimated the fraud to be worth $64.8 billion based on the amount in the accounts of Madoff's 4,800 clients as of November 30, 2008. Many clients found out that their entire retirement savings had been wiped out!

In most instances, large corporations totally understand the fallout and ramifications of unethical and sometimes borderline criminal behavior when chasing the dollar in an attempt to maximize corporate profits and meet or exceed stock investors expectations. In many situations, it is a decision based on risk verses return or increases in corporate profits.

Many corporate leaders and managers analyze the cost of the decisions that might bring harm to the public and lead to lawsuits that will award large punitive damages settlements. In most cases, when the potential profits greatly outweigh the possible payouts from punitive damages, a decision to proceed is made.

Unfortunately, when large corporations get caught breaking the law, the legal trouble can be severe. In some cases, the behavior is sanctioned by senior management. Whether the moral breach is within senior management or among the lower ranks of employees, the cost can be great and company stock prices may drop considerably.

One example of this behavior is Barclays PLC, an international bank. Barclays agreed to pay fines of $453 million, after US and UK regulators discovered that the bank was manipulating interest rates on consumer and corporate loans. As a result, Barclays fired the employees involved, and the chairman had to resign. Company shares dropped by more than 10%.

A second example took place at J & J, a pharmaceutical corporation that is responsible for manufacturing the drug Risperdal. An investigation into the marketing practices of J & J uncovered the fact that salespeople with the company were promoting Risperdal illegally to children and the elderly for unapproved purposes. Unfortunately, the drug has hormonal side effects in children and can be deadly for the elderly.

Even though many juries awarded the victims large punitive settlements, it didn't have a great impact when the company earned $206 billion from the sales of the drug. Setting aside $500 million or even $1 billion for punitive damages settlements seem like "business as usual" to these large corporations.

Some Encouraging Words

My concern and focus aren't your lifestyle or choices you are making. Whether you are engaging in deviant behaviors to earn a living or to avoid tax liabilities is none of my business. However, making you more conscious and aware of how you are spending your hard-earned money is my focus. When you are young, you often believe that the choices you are making and the behavior you are participating in will never result in consequences, but in reality, time catches up with all of us. Why not save and invest before you get caught in the act? Why not work yourself out of the deviant business that you are engaged in? A smart player will plan for the future and cease deviant business practices with their shirt on.

Whether engaging in deviant or non-deviant behaviors, my financial fitness program is designed to help you obtain financial success and the American dream of financial independence.

I understand more than most people that the struggle is real! That is why I am taking the time to write this book and get raw with the information regarding how money is spent and exchanged in our society. Unless you are born with a silver spoon in your mouth, obtaining the American dream of financial success is a day by day, step-by-step process that requires much time and commitment, but you can make it if you just get started on the right path–the younger, the better.

In my conclusions regarding deviant behavior and those who make their living on the black market, I remind you that I am not the one to judge you. Each individual person must live within the confines of their own consciousness. What is acceptable behavior to one person may or may not be acceptable to another person, but "to each their own!"

CHAPTER 8

Where do Americans Spend Their Money?

One day while on a radio broadcast together, my Jewish friend said to me, "all of the money in the ghetto is spent on chicken!" What I mean by chicken is disposable purchases on items and services that have little or no long–term value. Research supports the reality that many minorities and poor, disadvantaged people are the greatest consumers of disposable income purchases and services.

It is the psychology of money and spending habits. Low self-esteem causes many people to seek the purchases of goods and services that provide immediate gratification and satisfaction. These purchases are often symbolic of false financial success. A young lady said to me one day while sitting in my income tax office, "I may never own a house but all my children will be well dressed and my hair and nails will always be done!" It's this type of mentality that has perpetuated the unproductive spending habits of many minorities in the United States and even around the world in some cases. Research shows that blacks and Latinos make up the largest portion of this consumer group in the US.

I now better understand what my Jewish friend was trying to tell me. What he meant by saying "the money in the ghetto is spent on chicken" was that poor people tend to spend the majority of their money on items and services that have very little value or residual benefits. When you purchase an automobile, as soon as you drive it off the dealer's lot it begins to depreciate in value. I'm not against owning an automobile, but not at the expense of future savings and investments. Sometimes you have to crawl before you walk!

Status Purchases

The images that are portrayed on television and in the public media have a lot to do with the promotion of these types of purchases of goods and services. Singers and rappers in the entertainment business do not help the situation by establishing such purchases of goods and services as status symbols. Young people are very impressionable and easily influenced. Too much money in poor neighborhoods is spent on sneakers, designer clothes, gold and silver chains, bracelets, earrings, watches and rings, hair weaves, wigs, and automobile purchases, all of which have little or no long-term residual value. Why buy a Mercedes Benz when you don't have a garage to park it in? Too much money is spent on eating out verses home cooked meals. The Chinese take-out and other food establishments seldom go out of business in the poorest of American neighborhoods.

Even some Churches are guilty of exploiting the poor and needy through excessive requests for offerings and tithes. As a Christian, I am not against supporting the Church, but fiscal responsibility and budgeting should be an integral part of the Church's teachings and ministry, for it is a Biblical principle. The book of Proverbs 13:22 says "A good man leaves an inheritance to his children's children…" Financial exploitation in the Church begins with the notion that if I just be good in this life, I'll obtain success and blessings in the next life. This message causes many people to give up on financial success in this life while preparing for the next life.

I am aware of the New Testament words of Jesus when he said, "The poor will be with you always..." (Matthew 26:11), but the real question is why have some ethnic groups prospered while many blacks and Latinos stay in the same economic and financial position from generation to generation? When will we wake up and realize that it's not how much you make but what you do with your after-tax take-home income? If you always spend 100% or more of your net income you will never be worth more tomorrow than you are today. Unless you are born with a silver spoon in your mouth, for the majority of us, wealth building and financial success is a step–by–step process that is executed over time.

Please let me explain to you that I am not against the purchasing of disposable goods and services. Any successful budget should have a component of immediate gratification for some purchases. When an individual works all week and finally gets paid, it is human nature to want to reward yourself for your efforts. However, the problem begins when the purchases of these goods and services consume too much of the household budget. This is a problem shared by many minorities and in many cases, even non-minorities.

The solution is to limit these types of purchases. Too much money is being wasted at the expense of future savings and investments. If the individuals in this category would spend more time analyzing and budgeting their money in advance, they would see a pattern of behavior that is unhealthy for financial success and wealth building.

There is a concept that I would like to share with you at this time called *the law of diminishing returns*. This law states that the more you engage in a behavior or activity, the less joy or fulfillment you get out of it. For example, if you go out to eat dinner three times in one week, there is less joy and fulfillment in the third dinner as opposed to the first dinner. This is the concept behind the law of diminishing returns. Ask yourself this question, "how many times have you purchased goods or services that didn't give you fulfillment or meet your expectations?" You will find that in many cases, the more frequently you engaged in the purchase of goods or services, the less fulfillment you received.

If you had only planned in advance, you could have benefited from the joy and fulfillment generated by expectation. You see, there is a certain satisfaction that comes from expectation and anticipation. The fact that you know an activity or purchase is in your future can sustain your desires over a period of time. If I know that I have a dinner scheduled for the end of the week, the mere anticipation of this event can help me to stay on my budget and avoid unnecessary spending on other dinner plans within the same week.

Impulse Spending

Please understand that television and media spend millions of dollars on marketing of goods and services to persuade you to engage in what is known as *impulse spending*. Impulse spending is the act of purchasing goods and services based on an immediate reaction to some stimulus and not on pure consciousness of need. Everywhere you go, you will see billboards and advertisements geared towards convincing you to spend money on something. Unless you sit down and write out a well-structured budget with much thought and preparation, you will find that you are no match for the tactics used to provoke impulse spending.

Here is another example: are you aware that most products in grocery stores are displayed in a manner to cause you to purchase goods that you probably don't need? One of the worst habits you can develop is going food shopping when hungry. Many grocery stores strategically put the essential items in the back of the store, forcing you to travel past all the non-essential items before reaching the items that you really need. Even the colors of the labels of many products are chosen through scientific research to catch your eye and attention. Without proper planning, you are no match for the marketing industry.

Food products from popular brands may come in prettier packages, but that doesn't mean they're superior to their generic counterparts. While a 9-ounce box of Rice Krispies costs $4.79 at one New York City grocery store, its 12-ounce generic brethren costs only $1.98 with an identical list of ingredients. Part of the time we're not even buying brand names consciously, we're doing it because its familiar and we don't have to think about it. "Only $19.95! Call now and we'll double your order!" Such promises have lured in many unsuspecting consumers to what they thought was a great deal. The informercial industry brings in about $400 billion a year, according to the Electronic Retailing Association. But it's no secret that many impulses purchased go unused.

So, you are ready to begin that New Year's resolution to lose weight. You should think twice about joining a gym. We all come to the end of the year and say, "It's time to start getting in shape," but we don't think through whether we are willing to make the time commitment and if it is going to be worth the dollars we're spending. Unused gym memberships are not easy to cancel. Many no-show members are throwing away hundreds of dollars a year on gym memberships.

It is a good idea to think twice about purchasing bundled cable and phone services. Bundled packages aren't always a deal, especially if you're not using the extra services you're paying for. Consumers are often lured into bundled cable, internet, and phone packages because of the reduced rates offered during the first year. But paying for 500 channels that you're not watching, unlimited text messages, or airtime that you're not using is just a waste of money.

Another impulse use of service is withdrawing money from another bank's ATM. Using the closest ATM, rather than the one at your own bank, will typically cost you about $5. Most banks charge a fee for using third-party ATMs and the ATM you use also charges a fee.

These are just a few ways that impulse buying is marketed to lure money out of your pocket, but there are many more. Everywhere you go, the psychology of money is being used against you to draw the few dollars that you earn out of your pockets and into the purchases of disposable goods and services.

Where Americans Are Spending Their Disposable Income

African American men and women spend billions of dollars on their hair, but US beauty care companies are missing out. Most hair care products purchased by African Americans are imported from countries such as India and China, despite the US having one of the most lucrative hair care markets in the world. The market research firm Mintel values the black hair industry at more than $2.5 billion, but that statistic doesn't include products such as hair accessories, wigs or electric styling products. So, the industry is actually worth more. The hair care industry in total is currently estimated at $500 billion. That's more than double Greece's Gross Domestic Product.

Hair is an important aspect of the black female culture, so it's unsurprising that we potentially spend that much on it. Good Hair, the 2009 documentary by comedian Chris Rock, shined a spotlight on the business of black hair, particularly our use of relaxers and weaves and the sources of the extensions so many women sew into their hair. Since Rock's reveal of the industry, much both has and hasn't changed in the world of black hair.

In 2017, approximately $8.53 billion US dollars were spent on nail services in the US. A nail salon is a specialty beauty salon which provides nail enhancement services such as polishes, overlays, and extensions to both male and female customers.

The increase in spending on nail salon services in previous years has not corresponded with a growth in the number of nail salons across the United States. In 2006, there were approximately 59,842 nail salons in the US, and this number has oscillated over the years. In 2013, the figure dropped to 48,930; a decrease of over 10,000 salons. By 2015, the number of nail salons more than doubled to over 129,600 salons, only to drop to about 56,300 in 2017.

Salons can compete with one another by cost and range of services they offer. The share of services offered at nail salons and studios in the US was documented in 2014. In that year, 95% of salons offered pedicures and polish, making them the most common types of services. At the opposite end of the ranking came acrylic toenails with 36% and foot massages with 26% of salons offering these services. As manicures were deemed the most common type of service offered by nail salons, customers have to shop around when deciding which salon to use. The reputation of a particular nail technician may help this decision; so may the price. In 2017, the average price stood at $20.93, which is the highest since 2005. However, when it comes to the average price of deluxe manicures, customers were expected to pay up to $31.00 in 2017.

Although you might believe that the designer clothing business is very lucrative, it's not as much as you think. The average profit margin on designer clothing is 10%. Recent statistics show that the real lucrative market is in women's designer handbags and accessories. In 2017, the women's accessories market in the United States generated approximately $31.9 billion in retail sales.

As American fashion has slowly become more casual, so has footwear. That trend has become especially apparent in women's sneaker sales. Brands like Nike, Adidas, Dr Scholl's, Roxy, Puma, Steve Madden, and UGG are just a few of the names that are getting the benefit of women slipping into more comfortable footwear. Sneaker sales are growing as sales of high heels tumble! According to data from NPD Group, women's sneaker sales increased 37% in 2017, while high heels fell 11% during the same period.

The trend is twofold: consumers want comfort, and there are more options across all shoe categories. Athletic footwear grew by 2% in the US last year, generating nearly $20 billion in sales, according to NPD Group. Among women's leisure sneakers, Adidas and Nike drove almost half the growth in the segment. Another contender competing for the market share are designer sneakers. Rapper Kanye West and Stella McCartney both have collaborations with Adidas. Rap artist Kendrick Lamar has also teamed up with Nike. Rihanna's Puma line was so popular it sold out online.

In North America, Nike's largest market, revenue in the footwear sector amounted to about 9.32 billion dollars in 2018. The company saw strong growth, with sales up 9%, led by demand for both its shoes and apparel. More importantly, sales of its key Jordan line rose in the double digits, returning to "healthy sustainable growth in North America." In Europe, sales rose by 14% as Nike said it gained significant market share.

The average price for a pair of Nike sneakers is between $70 and $75. However, the average price for a pair of Air Jordan's is about $120 to $175. It costs less than $5 to produce Nike sneakers and running shoes. Nike manufacturing is done in countries with very low wages and little to no labor organizing or protection. Nike factory workers in Vietnam make $1.60 over a 10-hour day and Chinese workers make $1.75 in a 12-hour day. By 1992, Nike had eliminated all of their US work force in favor of low-wage Asian producers.

Under the category of bad habits, we will look at the revenue generated from sales and services in the gambling industry, the daily lottery, cigarette, drug, and alcohol consumption, pornography, and the Cannabis industry, just to name a few.

According to the American Gaming Association (AGA), the gaming industry in the US is worth $261 billion and supports 1.8 million jobs in 40 states. However, gambling has had a difficult history in the US, and it is only recently that the path is being cleared. Today, the industry enjoys rapid growth and increased revenue. Without the stigma it once had, it has become easier for people to access online gaming and betting. US gambling revenues reach over $150 billion every year. Now that sports betting is legal, many predict the total revenues for US betting each year will top $200 billion. Whether it's lottery tickets, slot machines, sport bets, bingo, or poker, Americans love to gamble. Below is a breakdown of the revenue generated by each form of betting for the year 2017.

- Commercial Casinos $41.2 billion
- Tribal Casinos $31.945 billion
- Poker Rooms $1.9 billion
- Lottery Revenues $80.55 billion
- Legal Bookmaking $248 million
- US Online Gambling $247.5 million
- Part-Mutuel $295 million
- Charitable Games/Bingo $2.15 billion

Total Revenue $158.54 billion

Americans love playing the lottery even though you have a better chance of being struck by lightning than you do of winning. According to North American Association of State and Provincial Lotteries, Americans spent a total of $73.5 billion on traditional lottery tickets in 2017. Add in electronic lottery games and that figure is $80 billion.

Lottery spending may be huge – but most Americans don't actually play, according to Victor Matheson, an economics professor at the College of Holy Cross and an expert on lotteries. Despite that fact, an average $325 a year is wagered on lottery tickets for every adult in the United States.

There is a lot of evidence to support the notion that lotteries draw on poor people. "A number of studies have investigated the demographics predictors of lottery gambling and have tended to find that, on average, state lottery products are disproportionately consumed by the poor," states a 2005 Brookings Institute paper. "Average annual lottery spending in dollar amounts is roughly equal across the lowest, middle, and highest-income groups. This implies that on average, low income households spend a larger percentage of their wealth on lottery tickets than other households."

When poor people gamble, a larger proportion have serious problems related to their gambling than wealthier people. Dean Gerstein, the principal investigator of the 1999 National Gambling Impact Study Commission report, told Politifact that "In general, gambling very heavily doesn't do nearly as much damage to rich people as it does to poor people because rich people can afford to throw away a lot more money on gambling without getting into hot water."

"The bottom line is a lot of this gambling is directed toward the poorer segments of society who are spending proportionately more," said John Kindt, a business administration professor at the University of Illinois who studies gambling. Kindt said he was speaking primarily about lotteries, that they are like a gateway drug to creating new addictive gamblers. "We are making poor people poorer."

As of a 2011, the US Center for Disease Control and Prevention reported that Americans spend $80 billion on cigarettes per year. It is not uncommon for a smoker to spend $70 a week, or $280 a month, on packs of cigarettes.

Bars and alcohol consumption are *money suckers*. A recent study revealed that people spent an average of $42.27 each time they went barhopping.

Spirit companies liquor sales rose 4% in the US in 2017, hitting a record $26.2 billion, fueled by high-end brown liquor and a big thirst for tequila and vodka according to industry groups. The Distilled Spirits Council, which represents companies such as Diageo PLC, Richard SA, and Brown-Forman Corp, said volumes rose 2.6% to 226 million 9-liter cases, reflecting millennials taste for high-end and super-premium blended scotch and whiskey products.

In the United States, vodka continued to be spirits' largest category, representing a third of all volume. Driven by more expensive brands such as Grey Goose and Ketel One, sales rose 3% to $6.2 billion in 2017. Among other liquors, American whiskey saw its sales rise 8.1%, while tequila rose 9.9% and Irish whiskey was up 12.8%. Rye whiskey saw the strongest growth, with demand rising 16.2% to 900,000 cases. Spirits also took market share away from beer for the eighth straight year, rising 0.7% to a 36.6% share of the total US alcoholic beverage market. For perspective, each percentage point of market share is worth $720 million in supplier sales revenue.

North America is a steady market in terms of growth and consumption of beer. It is the fourth-largest beer market in the world, which accounts for about 14% of global shares. In North America, beer is considered one of the most cherished alcoholic drinks, especially among the young. The North American beer market value is expected to reach $71.91 billion in 2018 and $98.08 billion by 2023.

The single largest marketplace for illegal drugs continues to be the US. Although the demand has decreased dramatically since its heyday in the mid-80s, close to 13 million Americans still think nothing about occasionally buying a gram of cocaine, a few hits of ecstasy, or a quarter ounce of weed to party with their friends on the weekends. A hard-core group estimated at between 5 and 6 million people have more serious drug habits and may spend $100 to $500 dollars a week on purchasing their drugs. These two groups – hard-core users and casual users – spend approximately $60 billion a year, according to US government estimates.

Imagine a typical weekend in New York City. Experts estimate that at least 1% of the population – 80,000 plus – spend $200 on illicit drugs. This alone amounts to $16 million a week or $832 million a year.

What keeps the drug industry going is the huge profit margins. Producing illicit drugs is a very cheap process. Like any commodities business, the closer you are to the source, the cheaper the product. Processed cocaine is available in Colombia for $1,500 per kilo and sold on the streets of America for as much as $66,000 a kilo. Heroin costs $2,600 per kilo in Pakistan but can be sold on the streets of America for $130,000 a kilo. Synthetics like methamphetamine are often even cheaper to manufacture, costing approximately $300 to $500 per kilo to produce in clandestine labs in the US and abroad and sold on the US streets for up to $60,000 per kilo.

The North American marijuana market posted $6.7 billion in revenue in 2016, up 30% from the year before, according to a new report from Arcview Market Research, a leading publisher of cannabis market research. The so-called *green rush* shows no sign of slowing down. Arcview projects sales will grow at a compound annual growth rate of 25% through 2026, when the North American market is expected to top $20.2 billion.

Despite the availability of free pornography on the internet, a detailed study done by Covenant Eyes showed that in 2005 and 2006, the US pornography industry generated $12.6 and $13.3 billion in revenue respectively. This encompassed video sales and rentals, internet, cable, pay-per-view, in-room, mobile, phone sex, exotic dance clubs, novelties, and magazines.

The fast food industry is booming in the United States. Fast food is mass-produced and designed for commercial resale with a strong priority placed on *speed of service* verses other relevant factors such as freshness, quality, or nutritional value. Fast food was originally created as a commercial strategy to accommodate the growing number of busy commuters, travelers, and wage workers who did not often have the time to sit down at a public house or diner and wait for their meal. By making speed of service the priority, this ensured that customers with strictly limited time were not inconvenienced by waiting for their food to be cooked on-the-spot. For those with no time to spare, fast food became a multibillion-dollar industry.

Listed below are the top 20 fast food chains in the US as of 2014.

20. Papa John's – Papa John's generated $2.7 billion in sales. Despite rising food prices, this pizza chain managed to stay on top. The brand partnered with influential celebrities and athletes like Peyton Manning, which contributed to its success.
19. Jack in the Box – Jack in the Box generated $3.2 billion in sales. The chain is known for selling breakfast all-day, which many

other fast food chains are not able to do. Jack in the Box maximized sales by capitalizing on late-night snackers.

18. Arby's – Arby's specializes in sliced meat sandwiches, generating $3.2 billion in sales in 2014.

17. Dairy Queen – Dairy Queen generated $3.2 billion in sales. The chain released a line of oven-baked sandwiches to complement their famous ice cream Blizzard.

16. Little Caesars – Little Caesars generated $3.2 billion in pizza sales. They received a top ranking from Sandelman and Associates for its "value and affordability" when compared to 148 other food chains.

15. Carl's Jr./Hardee's – Carl's Jr. purchased the Hardee's restaurant chain in the late 90s, allowing it to expand into the Midwest and the East Coast. The company generated $4.0 billion in sales in 2014.

14. Chipotle – Chipotle generated $4.0 billion in sales. Known for its quality ingredients, the company recently took Subway's spot as America's healthy fast food of choice. People obsess over the chain.

13. Sonic Drive-In – Sonic generated $4.1 billion in sales with its drive-in restaurant service.

12. Domino's – Domino's generated $4.1 billion in sales, primarily through their delivery service.

11. KFC – KFC's fried chicken and their "secret recipe of 11 herbs and spices" earned $4.2 billion in sales.

10. Panera Bread – Panera Bread operate "bakery-café fast casual" restaurants and generated $4.5 billion in sales.

9. Pizza Hut – A full-service pizza restaurant that also offers drive through and delivery service, Pizza Hut generated $5.5 billion in sales.

8. Chick-fil-A – Chick-fil-A generated $5.5 billion in sales specializing in high-quality chicken.

7   Dunkin Donuts – Dunkin Donuts generated $7.2 billion in sales and is the most consumed doughnut in the US.

6   Taco Bell – Taco Bell, one of only two Mexican-style restaurants on this list, generated $8.2 billion in sales.

5. Wendy's – Wendy's generated $8.5 billion in sales embracing a different strategy to boost sales in 2014 by targeting millennials.

4. Burger King – Burger King, once McDonald's closest rival, generated $8.6 billion in sales.

3. Subway – Subway generated $11.9 billion in sales after marketing itself as a healthier alternative to burgers and fries.

2. Starbucks – Starbucks generated $12.7 billion in sales. Starbucks is the leading coffee chain in the world.

1. McDonald's – McDonald's generated $35.4 billion in sales. McDonald's is one of the most popular fast-food chains and one of the top franchises in the world.

The total sales revenue generated by the top twenty fast food chains in 2014 was $143.5 billion dollars.

One item that has become a necessity to over 91% of all Americans is a cell phone. The revenue from smartphone sales is projected to amount to $88.9 billion in 2019 with the cost of a cell phone ranging from $60 to more than $1,000. Getting a cellphone is a new milestone for children. A new survey in Child Guide Magazine, a resource guide for parents, found that the average American child gets their first cell phone when they're six years old. The survey, which interviewed 2,290 American parents, found that 31% of children received a cell phone for security reasons, while 25% received one so that children could keep in contact with their family. Twenty percent of parents gave their children cell phones so they could keep up with their friends in school.

You've probably already figured this one out: cell phone bills are pricey. The average American is now shelling out around $110 per month on cell phone service. How much you pay will depend on several things, including how much data you use, how much your state charges in taxes, and if you are on a financing plan or buy your phone outright.

The US music industry grew 11.9% to $9.8 billion as of 2017, thanks to continuing explosive growth from streaming, which jumped 20% in 2019 to $8.8 billion. This marks the fourth consecutive year of double-digit growth for the industry, as streaming music sales have grown from $4 billion in 2016 and now comprise nearly 80% of US music industry revenues.

Driving streaming's growth, according to figures recently released by the Recording Industry Association of America, was a 42.4% increase from 2017's 35.3 million subscribers to 50.2 million today. On-demand models dominated revenue, contributing nearly $6.1 billion, a 29.7% increase over the prior year's total of $4.7 billion, while streaming satellite broadcast revenues totaled $1.2 billion, up 28.9% from the prior year. These totals include sound-exchange distributions as designated in the RIAA press release, as well as payments to label services like Pandora.

Survival Debt and Predatory Lending

When you go to the car dealer, the first thing that the sales representative tells you is how much of a down payment you will need to drive the automobile off the dealer's lot. In reality, the first thing that should be discussed is not the down payment but the interest rate on the outstanding balance. In most cases, when you calculate the interest and principle paid on the purchase, you will see that the total payout over time is much greater than the value of the asset you have purchased.

Usually the longer the pay–off period, the higher the interest rate on the loan.

So, you can see from the examples set before you that "the struggle is real!" Many people in this country and even around the world are just living from paycheck to paycheck. However, there is an even worse condition that has started to evolve in more recent years called *survival debt.*

More and more individuals and families are financing their current life-styles through a new avenue of expense called survival debt. If you are living a lifestyle at a level of expense greater than 100% of your income, then you must be financing your lifestyle through credit spend-ing. Never before in the history of finance have so many individuals and families financed household and personal expenses by using credit card debt. Recent statistics show a steep rise in the use of credit cards to finance such purchases as food, gasoline, and clothing. Many of these credit cards have a high interest rate on unpaid balances that exceed 30 days. It is not uncommon for individuals to carry $40,000 or more in credit card debt related to maintaining a lifestyle. Most individuals have several credit cards with balances in excess of $10,000.

If you always pay the minimum balance allowed for each month, you will never repay the outstanding balance on most credit cards. If you were to factor in the interest paid on most purchases, you would find that even purchases of discounted goods and services were no longer a discount when you add the interest paid over time.

One of the biggest problems plaguing low-income neighborhoods and families is *predatory lending practices.* Predatory lending is defined as any lending practice that imposes unfair or abusive loan terms on a borrower. It is also any practice that convinces a borrower to accept unfair terms through deceptive, coercive, exploitative, or unscrupulous actions for a loan that a borrower doesn't need, doesn't want, or can't afford. By definition, predatory lending benefits the lender and ignores or hinders the borrower's ability to repay the debt. These lending tactics often try to take advantage of a borrower's lack of understanding about loans, terms, or finances.

Predatory lenders typically target minorities, the poor, the elderly, and the less educated. They prey on people who need immediate cash for emergencies such as paying medical bills, making a home repair, or car payment. These lenders also target borrowers with credit problems or people who recently lost their job. This could disqualify them from conventional loans or lines of credit, even though they have substantial equity in their homes. Predatory lending can take the form of payday loans, car loans, tax refund anticipation loans, or any type of consumer debt.

Over the past several years, predatory lending practices have been prevalent in the area of home mortgages. Since home loans are backed by a borrower's real property, a predatory lender can profit not only from terms stated in his or her favor, but also from the sale of a foreclosed home if a borrower defaults.

While there is some dispute about what constitutes a predatory lending practice, a number of actions are specifically barred by law. These include failure to disclose information or disclosing false information, risk-based pricing, and inflated charges and fees. There are other predatory practices such as loan packing, loan flipping, asset-based lending, and reverse redlining.

Inadequate or false disclosures take place when the lender hides or misrepresents the true cost, risk, and/or appropriateness of a loan's term, or the lender changes the loan terms after the initial offer.

Risk-based pricing is the practice of tying interest rates to credit history. While not entirely unusual, predatory lenders abuse the practice by charging very high interest rates to high-risk borrowers who are most likely to default.

Inflated fees and charges are often included in appraisals, closing costs, document preparation fees, and more. These are much higher than those charged by reputable lenders and are often hidden in the fine print.

The process of loan packing bundles unnecessary products with a loan like credit insurance, which pays off the loan if a homebuyer dies. These fees are often added into the cost of the loan.

The process of loan flipping takes place when a lender encourages a borrower to refinance an existing loan into a larger one with a higher interest rate and additional fees. This often gets repeated and becomes one of the most common practices among predatory lenders: loan churning, where borrowers are forced into a relentless loan cycle in which they are constantly paying fees and interest, without noticeably reducing the principal amount owed on the loan. Loan churning works like this: the lender makes a loan the borrower can't afford. The borrower fails to pay the loan back on time, so the lender offers a new loan that includes another set of fees and interest. The borrower, already under stress for not repaying the first loan, agrees to the second loan and the loan-cycle churn has started.

The Consumer Financial Protection Bureau says that 94% of repeat payday loans – churning – happens within one month of the first loan and consumers using payday loans borrow an average of 10 times a year. The interest and fees amount to $2.1 billion for borrowers. Borrowers often end up paying $450 in interest alone for a $350 principal. It is commonplace among predatory lenders and something consumers with poor credit history should be on guard against.

Asset-based lending takes place when a borrower is encouraged to borrow more than they should when a lender offers to refinance based on their amount of home equity, rather than their income or ability to repay.

Reverse redlining is the practice of targeting limited-resource neighborhoods that conventional banks may shy away from. Everyone in the neighborhood is charged higher rates to borrow money, regardless of credit history, income, or ability to repay.

A balloon mortgage is often offered to a borrower by convincing them to refinance a mortgage with one that has lower payments upfront but excessive payments later in the loan term. When the balloon payments cannot be met, the lender helps to refinance again with another high interest, high fee loan.

One of the worst loans a borrower can get is one that has *negative amortization*. This occurs when a monthly loan payment is too small to even cover the interest, which gets added to the unpaid balance. It can result in a borrower owning substantially more than the original amount borrowed.

Be aware of loans that have *abnormal prepayment penalties*. A borrower who tries to refinance a home with one that offers better terms can be assessed an abusive prepayment penalty for paying off the original loan early. Prepayment penalties are meant to discourage borrowers from paying off a loan early because it deprives the lender of interest they expected to receive for the life of the loan. Prepayment penalties vary from lender to lender. Many are for 2% of the amount owed. Others are for the equivalent of six months of interest on the loan. Most prepayment penalties are based around the number of years you have been paying the mortgage and usually expire after three years.

The Truth and Lending Act requires lenders to provide a disclosure form to borrowers that include a box that the lender must check if a prepayment penalty is in play. The wording on the form says a penalty "may" be charged and that wording often confuses consumers. Some people will read that to mean "may not" or simply skip over it in hopes that it will never be enforced. The smarter practice is for the borrower to ask the lender for details on the amount of the penalty and how long the prepayment period is. Up to 80% of subprime mortgages have abnormally high prepayment penalties.

Subprime loans are made to borrowers with poor credit history and high chance of defaulting on the repayment. They have become popular again and are inciting debate on whether extending high-interest credit to mostly poor consumers is a good thing for the economy.

The credit reporting firm Equifax classifies subprime borrowers as people with a credit score under 620. Equifax says that more than 50 million consumer loans worth more than $189 billion were made to subprime customers in the early 2000s when it primarily was used to buy homes. Subprime mortgage lending peaked in 2005 with $625 billion in loans, leading to the economic collapse in 2008. Subprime lending in 2014 was just $4 billion.

It is not uncommon for a lender to add language to a loan contract regarding mandatory arbitration. The lender adds language that makes it illegal for the borrower to take future legal action for fraud or misrepresentation. The only option then for an abused borrower is arbitration, which generally puts the borrower at a disadvantage.

Protecting yourself against predatory lenders should be a top priority of every borrower. The best defense against predatory lenders lies in educating yourself about their deceptive practices. Be aware of unlicensed loan officers who may contact you through the mail, via the telephone, or door-to-door solicitations. Reputable lenders typically don't operate in this way. Make sure any lender you work with is licensed. Stay clear of lenders who promise that your loan will be approved regardless of your credit history or rating. You should get a copy of your credit report and have some idea of what you should qualify for. Do not let yourself be rushed into the loan process. Study the paperwork closely and don't sign anything you don't agree with or understand. Always question high interest rates and fees. Refuse to accept payments you know you cannot afford. Decline any additional services "packed' into the loan, like credit or health insurance. Do a comparison shop of similar loans.

Educate yourself and know the federal laws that protect consumers against predatory lenders. Chief among them is the Equal Credit Opportunity Act (ECOA). This law makes it illegal for a lender to impose a higher interest rate or higher fees based on a person's race, color, religion, sex, age, marital status or national origin. The Home Ownership and Equity Protection Act (HOEPA) protects consumers from excessive fees and interest rates. High cost loans are subject to additional disclosure requirements and restrictions. In addition, 25 states have anti-predatory lending laws, and 35 states limit the maximum prepayment penalty that a homeowner is required to pay.

Another form of predatory lending that is widely used by many people who find themselves cash strapped is known as a *payday loan*. Payday loans are unsecured cash advances for small amounts of money (usually less than $1,000) with very high interest rates and short-term repayment demands. A typical loan may be $500, which borrowers often need to cover essentials such as rent, utilities, food, or a medical bill. Though the name suggests loans are limited to a borrower's paycheck, lenders will sometimes issue loans if they are certain the borrower will soon have access to repayment cash.

Payday lenders offer cash-advance loans, check-advance loans, post-dated check loans, or deferred-deposit loans. They almost never check credit histories, making their loans easy to get, but interest rates are extremely high, and their customers are among the nation's least savvy borrowers. The Consumer Financial Protection Bureau (CFPB), a federal government agency, issued a report in 2014 that showed most payday loans are made to borrowers who renew their loans so many times they end up paying more in fees than the amount they originally borrowed. The average payday loan borrower spends $520 in fees for what originally was a $375 loan.

Borrowing costs can soar astronomically in a short amount of time. Cash-strapped borrowers will often return to the lenders saying that they don't have the money to repay the loan, something these lenders actually like to hear. They will offer an extension known as a rollover that will give you another two weeks to repay the loan with the caveat that you must pay another fee.

Payday lenders advertise on TV, radio, online, and through the mail, targeting working people who can't quite get by from paycheck to paycheck. Though the loans are advertised as helpful for unexpected emergencies, seven out of 10 borrowers use them for regular, recurring expenses such as rent and utilities.

Financial experts say online lenders can be risky. They might offer a loan, but you can't be sure if they will use your information for other purposes potentially opening the door to scam artists. Many of the online sites are information brokers, which gather your financial data and sell it to lenders.

According to the Community Financial Services Association of America, there are an estimated 18,600 payday advance locations nationwide that have extended $38.5 billion in credit to 19 million households.

In the United States, payday loan operators typically operate from storefronts in low-income neighborhoods. Their customers generally have poor credit and have no other access to money to cover urgent bills. Payday lenders use different methods for calculating interest rates, often demanding nearly 400% on an annualized basis. Though many people assume payday lenders charge high interest because they deal with high-risk customers, default rates are typically quite low. Many states now regulate payday loan interest rates and many lenders have withdrawn from states that do.

Payday lenders used to set up shop just beyond the perimeter of military bases, gouging soldiers and their families. To stop the practice, a 2007 federal law capped annualized payday loan interest at 36% for active-duty service personal and their families. Not surprisingly the lenders are moving elsewhere.

The decline in operations has cut deeply into the payday loan business. The nonprofit Center for Financial Services reported a steep decline in the storefront loan business that began in 2013, with revenue falling 23.4% from 2014 to 2015 alone. Revenue also fell by 22.5% for nonbank online payday loans in the same period. But as payday loan revenue declines, issuers of subprime credit cards have made big gains, keeping the level of all subprime consumer lending relatively constant in the past several years.

The simplicity of borrowing and the easy access to cash make payday lending appealing to many customers, mostly those who have little or no access to conventional credit. Payday lenders rely on repeat customers, often low-income minorities, charging exorbitant compounding interest for cash advances. They seldom offer borrowers workable repayment plans, and in many states, operate with few regulations.

Payday lenders are subject to the federal Truth and Lending Act. It requires that lenders disclose the cost of the loan. Payday lenders must disclose the finance charges and the annual interest percentage rate (APR) in writing before you sign for the loan.

In spring 2018, the Federal Office of the Comptroller of the Currency, which regulates national banks, announced that banks would be able to write loans smaller than $5,000 and not be subject to standard underwriting rules. The goal is to extend bank lending to people whose credit makes it impossible to qualify for conventional loans or credit cards. Banks used to make loans like this called deposit advances, which were generally repaid quickly—often before a borrower's next paycheck. But new banking rules ended the practice in 2014 after regulators warned that deposit advances sometimes led borrowers to crippling debt. The 2018 revision will allow banks to return to the practice, but perhaps not for long. The CFPB is scheduled to impose strict regulations on loans of 45 days or less. However, in June 2018, the bureau's acting director said he would like to reevaluate that rule.

Below is a summary of the reasons why you should avoid payday loans:

- Payday loans are very expensive – High interest credit cards might charge borrowers an APR of 28 to 36%, but the average payday loan's APR is commonly 398% or more.
- Payday loans are financial quicksand – Many borrowers are unable to repay the loans in the typical two-week repayment period. When it is due, they must borrow or pay another round in fees, sinking them deeper and deeper into debt.
- Payday lenders want the right to access your bank account – They say it will save you the hassle of writing the commonly used post-dated check. But if the loan comes due and the funds aren't in your account, the payday lender can make repeated

attempts to withdraw the money, often resulting in multiple overdraft charges of $35 or more.

- Payday lenders can be ruthless debt collectors – If you can't repay the loan, prepare for a barrage of tactics that include late night calls from debt collectors

If you've never heard of a Refund Anticipation Loan or RAL, it's probably a good thing. RALs, also known as *instant refunds*, are short-term loans that are made based on the notion that you will be receiving a tax refund from the IRS. But they come at a significant price in terms of fees and interest, and the cost in most cases outweigh these benefits.

With an RAL, a tax preparer will offer you immediate payment of your refund, but in exchange you will receive less money than you are entitled to. The incentive for you is supposed to be the immediate receipt, so you won't have to wait for the IRS to issue you a refund check or deposit the money into your account. The tax preparer is then entitled to the full amount of your tax refund.

So, what are you actually paying for with these RAL services? The fees are ultimately similar to those charged for payday or auto title loans, which are widely referred to as predatory loans. The RAL loans are offered at high interest rates, ranging from about 40% to over 700% APR. In 2006, a study sanctioned in part by the Consumer Federation of America found that a consumer utilizing one of these RAL loans will likely pay approximately $100 for a refund of approximately $2,150. Although IRS regulations dictate that fees may not be related to the amount of your anticipated return, these figures indicate that in effect, the impatience of not being able to wait sometimes only one additional week may cost 5% or more of a taxpayer's return.

While the fees may appear minimal in comparison to the size of the refund, an RAL can be incredibly expensive once you consider the time frame in which you actually use the loan. With E-filing and all the available IRS partnerships that help consumers E-file for free, taxpayers can receive their tax refunds within three weeks and as quickly as ten to fourteen days if they choose to receive their refund via direct-deposit.

According to the National Consumer Law Center (NCLC), 12 million taxpayers used an RAL in 2004. Despite numerous attempts by the IRS to change the refund anticipation loan system, they have thus far been unsuccessful. The concerns that have been expressed by the NCLC are that many tax preparers do not adequately educate their customers about RAL. Many taxpayers have no idea when they might expect to receive their refund, and most do not understand the fees associated with their loans. Even some of the largest tax preparers have been accused of predatory lending practices, including H & R Block, who in 2002 settled a suit brought by the New York City Department of Consumer Affairs for RAL lending procedures. These tax refund anticipation loans are just another form of predatory lending practice, so steer clear of them.

Auto title loans are a form of predatory lending also. If you're strapped for cash and your is car free and clear, an auto title loan might seem like a good way to get some fast cash when you need it. But auto title loans are among the most expensive kinds of credit you can get along with payday loans and pawnshops.

Auto title loans use your car as collateral. Collateral is property that's used to secure the loan on time. The lender has the right to take whatever property is listed as collateral for the loan. That's right: If you don't repay your auto title loan, the lender can take your car. Some auto title lenders will even require you to install a GPS device in your car so that if they decide to repossess the vehicle, they can find you wherever you go.

Auto title loan lenders charge an average of 25% per month in interest on the loan. That's an annual percentage rate (APR) of 300%! Even credit cards only charge an average APR of 15.59%, and they're the most expensive traditional credit option. And you can expect an auto title loan to include a variety of fees on top of the exorbitant interest. In other words, if you were to take out a $1,000 auto loan and repay it 30 days later, you'd owe the lender $1,250, plus who knows how much in fees.

If you decide that you truly have no other option but to get an auto title loan, shop around with different title lenders to get the best deal you can. Review the loan terms carefully and decline any add-on features such as roadside assistance. If the lender insists that you take such add-ons, find a different lender. Ask about all the different fees listed on the loan documentation (there will likely be several) and try to negotiate to get those fees removed or at least reduced. If you push the lender hard-enough, they may be willing to bend a little on those costs. Finally, steer clear of rollover offers. Title lenders will often allow you to pay just the interest on your loan and roll over the principal to a new loan but doing so will trap you in the endless cycle of escalating fees and interest.

The auto title loan business is very lucrative. If you put $100,000 to work at 8% per month with an average loan principal of $4,000, a measly 25 title loans earn $8,000/month in interest. The typical car title loan is 8 months in duration. You can see there is some serious cash to be made! You can run this out of a 300 sq. ft. office with one or two employees at $10/hr. Basically, you need a phone, a desk, and a sign. After a few years, it's nothing for a very small operator to have $2 million on the street at 8% interest per month.

While the practices of predatory lenders may not always be illegal, they can leave victims with ruined credit, burdened with unmanageable debt, or homeless. These practices, either individually or in concert with each other, create a cycle of debt that causes severe financial hardship on families and individuals.

Credit Card Habits

For credit-card issuers, lending to so-called subprime borrowers has become a revenue driver since the Great Recession. Nearly 50 million Americans, including more than 30 million millennials, have poor credit and are considered "deep subprime consumers," according to the annual Consumer Credit Card Report by personal finance website NerdWallet.

"There's a big difference between a credit score of 600 and 800," said Sean McQuay, a credit card analyst at NerdWallet. "Consumers with excellent credit have access to the best loan terms and lowest insurance rates, as well as the most options." It's a difference of thousands of dollars in interest and fees per year!

It's no secret that subprime borrowers face more expensive credit terms. While the average annual percentage rate for all borrowers is 18.2%, those with credit scores below 630 are charged 22.2% on average, according to McQuay.

That translates into more revenue for card issuers. While fees are paid by credit-card holders across the board, interest is charged only to those who carry a balance, which are cardholders with poor credit according to a report by the Consumer Financial Protection Bureau. The interest payments all cardholders make account for 80% of the total revenue card issuers receive from consumers, the CFPB report said.

But while those considered prime borrowers are generally paying down debt, riskier consumers have been increasing their card balances up to $5,063 on average, up from $4,891 one year earlier, according to a separate study from credit-scoring company TransUnion (based on 2016 statistics). As a result, card issuers continue to increase the availability of credit, particularly to millennials and other consumers with lower credit scores. About 10 million new consumers entered the credit-card marketplace in the last year alone, the majority of which were subprime borrowers, according to TransUnion.

Although credit card use is rising, Jess Sharp, executive director of the American Bankers Association's Card Policy Council, said that is a result of an improving economy and that credit-card debt remains manageable.

"While more consumers are using credit cards for short-term financing, the amount of credit-card debt they are carrying relative to their disposable income is quite low by historical standards," he said in a statement.

For those just starting out, or who have low credit scores or limited credit histories, McQuay recommends opting for a secured card. Although these cards require a security deposit, typically in the range of $300 to $500, an amount that is usually equal to the credit limit, the deposits are fully refundable when the account is closed or when the consumer upgrades to an unsecured card.

The upside is that it gives consumers access to credit without needing a co-signer, while steering clear of subprime specialist issuers who market specifically to borrowers with bad credit and charge high fees and interest to mitigate their risk. "Many of the largest issuers do offer secured cards but they're not heavily marketed because they're not money makers for banks," McQuay said.

For those who want an unsecured card, McQuay advises consumers to choose one with a high limit over a low APR, with the goal of paying the bill in full every month to avoid interest charges. That way, consumers can maximize their debt-utilization ratio, which is the amount borrowed compared to the total credit available. The debt-utilization ratio is a big component of a credit score, so having a high limit but keeping a balance low can help consumers save on interest and eventually boost their credit scores.

March of 2018 saw the sixth rise of the federal funds interest rate – and thus, the US Prime Rate – since 2015, a marker of the continued growth of the US economy since its lows in the late 2000s. But while economists may hail the increase as a positive sign, average consumers may not feel so positive about an increase in their interest rates – particularly not the 50% of consumers with credit card debt that just got more expensive. And we're not talking about an insignificant amount of debt, either. Total revolving debt in the US has reached an all-time high, coming in just a little under $1.03 trillion by the end of January.

Of the more than $1 trillion worth of revolving debt balances Americans carried in 2018, the vast majority is credit card debt. The total amount of credit card debt balances hit $830 billion at the end of 2017. While not an all-time high, the $26 billion jump to $830 billion was the third such increase in 2017, resulting in a total annual increase of $50 billion since the end of 2016.

Given the 126.2 million American households, the average household has around $8,161 in revolving debt, approximately $6,577 of which is credit card debt. With nearly 248 million Americans over the age of 18, that comes out to a total of $3,353 in credit card balances per US adult.

Of course, not every consumer carries a credit card. Only around 70% of Americans have at least one card, which amounts to about 173 million cardholders over the age of 18. The average card holder has approximately $4,789 in credit card balances.

Around 29% of cardholders make low payments at or near the minimum payment most months, but it's not always the consumers you think it will be. For example, while those with FICO credit scores above 700 are certainly more likely to pay their full credit card balance every cycle, even those with scores above 800 will make a low payment around 20% of the time.

Overall, the amount of debt seems to be the best indicator of how much is paid, with balances under $1,500 more likely to be paid in full, and those over $2,000 more likely to receive just the minimum payment. Other patterns in the data emerge when looking at factors like income, age and region.

The correlation between income and credit card debt seem to show that money doesn't necessarily buy debt freedom. In fact, average credit debt appears to increase with annual income, and those with the largest income have the highest credit card balances. Credit card debt may also be a factor of household net worth at both ends of the spectrum. Households whose net worth is $0 carry the most debt overall.

As might be expected, those with the highest incomes – $150,000+ annually – are the most likely to pay their credit card balance in full each month. However, they may still make minimum or near-minimum payments as much as 38% of the time. In comparison, those with incomes less than $50,000 will make low payments about 50% of the time. Cardholders with income less than $25,000 are the least likely to pay in full.

While not as obvious a factor as income, age also seems to be a correlating element, with older consumers and middle-aged consumers more likely to pay their credit cards in full. A good portion of the correlations between age and credit debt is likely due to the cost of living, as those in their middle-adult years are more likely to have home-related expenses and have dependents than those in older and younger demographics. Homeowners tended to pay twice as much credit card interest per year as renters.

Experian's data – which arguably is bound to be the broadest – says that men and women both have an average revolving debt ratio of 29.9%, though women have 3.7% less average debt than their male counterparts. Women also tend to have better credit scores.

The Midwest and Great Lakes regions seem to be where to find the most responsible credit card users, home to both the lowest average credit card debts and the highest average credit scores (which belong to Iowa and Minnesota, respectively).

Student Loans

Furthering your education could be one of the smartest decisions you can make but think twice about attending a school of higher education. Unless you were fortunate to have parents who set up an educational fund when you were very young, you will most likely need to finance your education expense with student loans provided by the federal government and other lending institutions. Student loan debt in 2018 hit a crisis level of $1.5 trillion!

Student loan debt is now the second highest consumer debt category – behind only mortgage debt – and higher than both credit cards and auto loans. According to Make Lemonade, there are more than 44 million borrowers who collectively owe $1.5 trillion in student loan debt in the US alone. The average student in the class of 2016 has $37,172 in student loan debt. The current student loan delinquency or default rate is 10.7% (that's over 90 days delinquent).

Are you financially prepared to be a parent?

A 2018 study reported the average cost of raising a child born in 2015 over 18 years (not including college) was estimated at $233,610. So, the next time your boyfriend, partner, or husband asks you about having a child, ask them "are you willing to set aside $233,610 of your current and future income so that our child can enjoy an average lifestyle?"

The report is based on middle-class families. Middle-class families are defined as having a before-tax income of $59,200 to $107,000. Families with lower incomes are expected to spend $174,690, while families with higher incomes will likely spend $372,210.

One of the largest expenses relating to raising a child is childcare services. This may not come as a surprise to many parents, but families spend big bucks on basic childcare services. A recent Care.com report found the majority of American households spend more than 10% of their household income on childcare, and a fifth of households more than a quarter of their income.

Just how much are they spending? Nationally, the average cost for a week at a childcare center for a single child totaled $196. An after-school sitter set the average family back $214 for 15 hours of work a week. Hiring a nanny topped $556 a week.

Religious Institutions and Donations

A new analysis from Georgetown University that attempts to document the economic value of religion in US society found that the faith sector is worth $1.2 trillion, more than the combined revenue of the top 10 technology companies in the country including Apple, Amazon, and Google. This estimate includes the fair market value of goods and services provided by religious organizations and the contributions of businesses with religious roots. Just the revenues of faith-based organizations came to $378 billion annually. If the household income of Americans who practice a religion is taken into account, the estimated value of the faith sector is $4.7 trillion.

When people donate to religious groups, it's tax-deductible. Churches don't pay property taxes on their land or buildings. When they buy things, they don't pay sales taxes. When they sell things at a profit, they don't pay capital gains tax. If they spend less than they take in, they don't pay corporate income taxes. Priest, ministers, rabbis, and the like get *parsonage exemptions* that let them deduct mortgage payments, rent, and other living expenses from their income taxes. They also are the only group allowed to get out of Social Security taxes (and benefits).

Recent research identified the following eight pastors to be the richest in America by net worth:

1. Kenneth Copeland $760 million
2. Pat Robertson $100 million
3. Benny Hinn $42 million
4. Joel Osteen $40 million
5. Creflo Dollar $27 million
6. Billy Graham $25 million
7. Rick Warren $25 million
8. Joyce Meyer $8 million

There is no end to analyzing where Americans spend their hard-earned income, but we have tried to give you an idea of some of the most popular purchases of goods and services. How to keep up with current fashions and trends, eat out a few times a month, enjoy the latest gadgets and electronic devises, support your habits, have a family, go to church, and still have money left to invest in your future is a challenge that most American are failing miserably to do.

Invisible Taxes

Now let us take a look at another category of expense that you may or not be conscious of. It is the taxes that you pay on goods and services! Whether you file an annual tax return or not you are still paying taxes to the government on a daily basis. Taxes generated from working people's income is not the only way the government gets its share of revenue. Let us spend a little time looking at the taxation of goods and services paid for on a daily basis by most Americans.

The sales tax is most often used as a method for states and local governments to raise revenue. Purchases made at the retail level are assessed a percentage of the sales price of a particular item. Rates vary between jurisdictions and the type of item bought. For example, a pair of shoes may be taxed at one rate, restaurant food at another, while some items, like staple commodities bought at a grocery store, may not be taxed at all. The same shoes may be taxed at a different rate if sold in a different state or county.

Some believe that sales taxes are the most equitable form of taxation, since they are essentially voluntary, and they extract more money from those who consume more. Others believe that they are the most regressive form of taxation, since poorer people wind up paying a larger portion of their income in sales tax than wealthier individuals.

Excise taxes are based on the quantity of an item and not on its value. For example, the federal government imposes an excise tax of 18.4 cents on every gallon of gas purchased, regardless of the price charged by the seller. States often add an additional excise tax on each gallon of fuel.

User fees are taxes that are assessed on a wide variety of services, including airline tickets, rental cars, toll roads, utilities, hotel rooms, licenses, financial transactions, and many others. Depending upon where someone lives, a cellphone, for example, may have as many as six separate user taxes running up the monthly bill by as much as 20%.

So-called sin taxes are imposed on items like cigarettes and alcohol. Luxury taxes are imposed on certain items such as expensive cars or jewelry.

Of the three forms of state taxes – sales, property, and income – the sales tax hurts the poor most. State sales taxes are highly "regressive." That is, they end up taking a larger chunk of change from people that have smaller sums of money and slower income growth.

Let's say that a rich person and a poor person each spend $100 on taxable grocery items. This $100 expenditure – and the sales tax on that $100 – both deal heavier blows on the poor person's income because it's smaller. As a share of their income, the poor pay a 7% rate on sales and excise taxes, while middle-income families pay a 4.7% rate, and the wealthy pay less than 1%, on average.

Understandably, then, low-income Americans living in states that rely more on sales tax are worse off. In Washington State, for example, the poor pay nearly 17% of their income in state taxes, while the rich only pay 2.4%. On the other hand, in D.C. and California, more reliance on personal income taxes and better earned income tax credit policies make the tax system more equitable (though even there, low and middle-income groups pay higher proportions of their comparatively smaller incomes).

Listed below are the 10 most Regressive state and local tax systems:

Rank	State	Poorest 20%	Middle 60%	Top 1%	Poor vs Top 1%
1	Washington	16.8%	10.1%	2.4%	686%
2	Florida	12.9%	8.3%	1.9%	666%
3	Texas	12.5%	8.8%	2.9%	435%
4	South Dakota	11.3%	7.9%	1.8%	616%
5	Illinois	13.2%	10.9%	4.6%	289%
6	Pennsylvania	12.0%	10.1%	4.6%	286%
7	Tennessee	10.9%	8.4%	3.0%	365%
8	Arizona	12.5%	9.5%	4.6%	272%
9	Kansas	11.1%	9.2%	3.6%	310%
10	Indiana	12.0%	10.6%	5.2%	231%

Now let us take a look at the industry that will mostly likely be the next to be taxed. That is the marijuana industry. The use of marijuana is becoming legal in more and more states as time moves on. A recent study shows that marijuana tax collections in Colorado and Washington have exceeded initial estimates.

A mature marijuana industry could generate up to $28 billion in tax revenues for federal, state, and local governments, including $5.5 billion from business taxes and $1.5 billion from income and payroll taxes. A federal tax of $23 per pound, similar to the federal tax on tobacco, could generate $500 million per year. Alternatively, a 10% sales surtax could generate $5.3 billion per year, with higher tax rates collecting proportionally more.

So, in our conclusion on the taxation of goods and services, we see that once again the poor carry the heaviest burden. The people who can least afford these taxes are the very ones who spend the greatest percentage of their income paying these taxes. In many cases, these taxes are not visible and are hidden and buried in charges for goods and services. Very few of the poorest people take the time to analyze the various taxes that they pay on regular purchases of goods and services. Whether it is a soda, fast food purchase, or cell phone payment, these taxes are everywhere!

CHAPTER 9

Wealth Building: A Step by Step process

Until you understand the value of one dollar... you will never be worth more tomorrow than you are today.

For most Americans, wealth building will be a step by step process, a daily or weekly ritual. As I have often said, "It's not how much you make, but what you do with it" that will determine the final outcome. It is so very important to understand that taking the first step is the hardest thing to achieve. Most people say, "I don't make enough money to save. If I can just make more money, I can start to save."

When you speak these words, you are missing the most essential point. Life is about choices. It is not until much later in life that you understand that the expenses and purchases you made, spending 100% or more of your take-home income during your youthful years, do not bring value or replace the pain and suffering of not saving and investing in your senior years after retirement.

Just about anyone, regardless of income level, can change their financial position over time. Changing your financial situation is not rocket science. There are only two roads that lead to a change in financial position. You must either increase income or decrease expenses. The best route is a combination of both. In most but not all cases decreasing expenses should be the first choice and starting point. Increasing income might not be an immediate opportunity, but it should always be a long-term goal.

Before you can take a step on the road to change your current financial position, you need to know your current financial situation, where you are, and what your opportunities and options are. You need a well-thought-out written plan of action.

There are so many opportunities and vehicles that can help you on the road to increasing income. Some require a substantial investment while others require only a minimum investment of capital to get started. Some have a greater risk factor, while others are more conservative with a much lower level of risk. Usually, the greater the risk, the greater the return, but not in all cases. Your age and risk tolerance should be factored into your decision.

Actually, it is not as hard as you think to change your current financial position. With the age of computers and search engine technology, recent advancements have more than leveled the playing field. There are opportunities to grow and communicate business ideas at a level that never existed before.

Unless you were blessed to be born into a family with money, you are like the majority of Americans, and wealth building is a day by day, step by step process over time.

Unfortunately, there is a big misconception regarding how much you need to earn in order to begin saving and investing. In reality, just about anyone of any income bracket can effectively save and invest at any time. It is not so much the level of income that you earn, but the level of self-discipline that you practice.

There have been instances where homeless people living on the street and receiving a minimum social security or public welfare check have been found deceased with as much as $200,000 on their personal body. By saving every penny of their monthly check over many years and years of begging, they amass a great savings.

Now this is not the conventional method of saving nor the norm, but only an example of strong commitment and determination along with a high level of self-discipline.

The very first step on the road to wealth building is to grasp and understand the power of consistent week by week, month by month saving and investing. It is paramount that you saturate yourself with the concept that it's not the amount that you set aside, but the consistent process over time that will yield you a return and change your financial position.

A very simple example can help you to better understand the concept. If you were to begin saving and investing $25 every month over a 20-year period and earning 3% interest on your investment, after 20 years you would have $8,228. This is a very simple example, and a 3% return on your investment is extremely easy to obtain. The number one key is to start the saving and investment process as young as possible (although, you are never too old to start; better late than never). The second key is to understand the importance of consistency over time.

Building wealth is a topic that can spark heated debate, promote quirky "get rich quick" schemes, or drive people to pursue transactions they might otherwise never consider. But are three simple steps to building wealth a misleading concept? The simple answer is *no*. But while the basic steps to building wealth are simple to understand, they're much more difficult to follow.

Basically, to accumulate wealth over time, you need to do three things.

1. Make money. Before you can begin to save or invest, you need to have a long-term source of income that's sufficient to have some left after you've covered your necessities and debts.
2. Save money. Once you have an income that's enough to cover your basics, develop a proactive savings plan.
3. Invest money. Once you've set aside a monthly savings goal, invest it prudently.

This makes a simple equation:

$$income = controlled\ spending/savings + investments$$

Understanding Three Simple Steps to Building Wealth

Step One: Make Enough Money

This step may seem elementary, but for those just starting out or in transition, this is the most fundamental step. Most of us have seen tables showing that a small amount regularly saved and compounded over time can eventually add up to substantial wealth. But those tables never cover the other side of the story. Are you making enough to save in the first place?

Keep in mind that there's only so much you can cut in costs. If your costs are already cut down to the bone, you should look into ways to increase your income. Also, are you good enough at what you do, and do you enjoy it enough that you can do it for 40 or 50 years and save that money?

There are two basic types of income—earned and passive. Earned income comes from what you "do for a living," while passive income is derived from investments. Those beginning their careers or in a career change can start with four considerations to decide how to derive their earned income:

1. What do you enjoy? You will perform better and be more likely to succeed financially doing something you enjoy.
2. What are you good at? Look at what you do well and how you can use those talents to earn a living.
3. What will pay well? Look at careers that involve what you enjoy and pay well enough to meet your financial expectations.
4. How to get there? Determine the education, training, and experience requirements needed to pursue your options.

Taking these considerations into account will put you on the right path. The key is to be open-minded and proactive. You should also evaluate your income situation periodically, at least once a year.

Step Two: Save Enough Money

You make enough money, you live pretty well, but you're not saving enough. What's wrong? The main reason this occurs is that your wants exceed your budget. To develop a budget or to get your existing budget on track, try these steps:

1. *Track your spending for at least a month.* You may want to use a financial software package to help you do this. Make sure to categorize your expenditures. Sometimes being aware of how much you spend can help you control your spending habits.

2. *Trim the fat.* Break down your wants and needs. The need for food, shelter, and clothing are obvious, but also address less obvious needs. For instance, you may realize you're eating lunch at a restaurant every day. Bringing your own lunch to work two or more days a week can help you save money.

3. *Adjust according to your changing needs.* As you go along, you probably will find that you've over- or under-budgeted a particular item and need to adjust.

4. *Build your cushion.* You never really know what's around the corner. Aim to save around three to six months' worth of expenses. This prepares you for financial setbacks, such as a job loss or health problem. If saving this cushion seems daunting, start small.

5. *Get matched!* Contribute to your employer's 401(k) or 403(b), and try to get the maximum your employer is matching.

The most important step is to distinguish between what you really need and what you merely want. Finding simple ways to save a few extra bucks here and there could include programming your thermostat to turn itself down when you're not home, using regular gasoline instead of premium, keeping your tires fully inflated, buying furniture from a quality thrift shop, and learning how to cook.

This doesn't mean you have to be thrifty all the time. If you're meeting savings goals, you should be willing to reward yourself and splurge (an appropriate amount) once in a while. You'll feel better and be motivated to make more money.

Step Three: Invest Money Appropriately

You're making enough money and saving enough, but you're putting it all in conservative investments like the regular savings account at your bank. That's fine, right? Wrong! If you want to build a sizable portfolio, you have to take on some risk, which means you'll have to invest in securities. So how do you determine what's the right level of exposure for you?

Begin with an assessment of your situation. The CFA Institute advises investors to build an investment policy statement. To begin, determine your return and risk objectives. Quantify all of the elements affecting your financial life, including household income, your time horizon, tax considerations, cash flow or liquidity needs, and any other factors unique to you.

Next, determine the appropriate asset allocation for you. Most likely you will need to meet with a financial advisor unless you know enough to do this on your own. This allocation should be based on your investment policy statement. Your allocation will most likely include a mixture of cash, fixed income, equities, and alternative investments.

Risk-averse investors should keep in mind that portfolios need at least some equity exposure to protect against inflation. Also, younger investors can afford to allocate more of their portfolios to equities than older investors because they have time on their side.

Finally, diversify. Invest your equity and fixed-income exposures over a range of classes and styles. Do not try to time the market. When one style (e.g., large-cap growth) is underperforming the S&P 500, it is quite possible that another is outperforming it. Diversification takes the timing element out of the game. A qualified investment advisor can help you develop a prudent diversification strategy.

Now that we have shared with you the basic framework of step by step wealth building, let us take a more detailed look at the process.

Create a Spending Plan

First, you need to have a plan for your money. When you don't know where your money is coming from and where it's going, it's difficult to direct it in a way that benefits you. Take a step back and make a plan for your money. Know your income, your expenses, how much is earmarked for additional expenses, and how much is for other financial goals.

The wealthy see money as a resource and a tool. They have plans for the money, and they know how money works to help them build wealth over time. Consider your financial goals and create a spending plan likely to help you reach them.

Spend Wisely

Building wealth doesn't have to be about hoarding all your money and never having any fun until you're too old to truly enjoy yourself. Instead, part of wealth building is learning how to spend on the things that matter to you. Think about your values and priorities and focus on those items when you make your spending plan.

If going on vacation, saving for your child's college, or giving to charity is important to you, include those items in your spending plan. However, if you don't care whether you watch the latest show, don't spend money on a huge TV. If it's not important to you to have a big house, keep your mortgage small.

There's no right or wrong answer to your spending. Only you can decide what matters to you. However, when you stop spending on things that don't matter to you, you might be surprised at how quickly you can build wealth.

Pay Off High-Interest Debt

High-interest debt does nothing for you. As you pay interest for the privilege of maintaining that debt, your financial resources are being diverted away from the things likely to help you build wealth. While some types of low-interest or tax-deductible debt can help you along the way, high-interest debt rarely has a good purpose.

Pay down your high-interest debt as quickly as possible so you can start putting that money to better use building wealth for you – not someone else.

Create an Emergency Fund

Have a plan to handle emergencies. An emergency fund can be a good way to plan for the unexpected without the need to turn to debt. There's a widely publicized stat from the Federal Reserve that indicates almost half of Americans couldn't handle a $400 emergency without resorting to debt. You don't want to be one of those statistics.

How you structure your emergency fund is up to you. For those with higher risk tolerance, the idea of placing some of the money in a high-yield savings account for easy access while putting the bulk of the emergency fund in a taxable investment account makes sense. You can grow your funds faster that way.

Carefully think about what you can handle, and what makes sense for your financial situation. No matter how you do it, you want a stash of capital you can draw on in an emergency.

Earn More Money

Too often, when we talk about saving and building wealth, we focus on cutting costs. However, sometimes what's really needed is more money. If you want to build wealth, you can't just focus on cutting back. You can't focus on scarcity.

Instead, look for ways to earn more money. If you work for a company, make yourself valuable so you're eligible for raises and promotions. When you're not being adequately compensated, look for a new job that pays more and recognizes your worth. It's also possible to start a business or side hustle to make more money. Your side business might grow into a solid money-maker down the road. Even if it doesn't, you can put the money you make to work, helping you build future wealth.

Invest

The importance of investing while you build wealth can't be stressed enough. Few of us have the financial resources to effectively grow our wealth using only a savings account. Instead, the compounding returns that come with investing are necessary to build substantial wealth over time.

Start with a tax-advantaged retirement account through your job or open an IRA. Tax-advantaged investment accounts help your money grow more efficiently and can make a big difference down the road. However, don't neglect taxable investment opportunities. Whether you invest in the stock market, real estate, or other assets, investing can help you grow your wealth faster than letting it sit in a savings account.

Protect Your Assets with Insurance

Finally, don't forget to protect your assets with the right insurance. Asset protection isn't sexy, but it is necessary. The right health insurance can keep you from completely depleting your accounts to pay for a hospital visit, while homeowners insurance protects you from the costs associated with the loss of your biggest asset.

Think about how much it would cost in a lump sum if you had to pay to replace a car, or what would happen if you needed to use money to support your family if you suffered a temporary disability. The right insurance coverage can reduce your financial risk, leaving you free to build wealth with money that would otherwise go toward replacing losses.

Implement and adjust as needed. Know where you spend your money, spend it wisely, avoid high-interest debt, have a rainy-day fund, increase your income, and invest and protect your assets with insurance to avoid catastrophic losses. Each of these is a simple concept, but that doesn't mean they are simple to put in place overnight. But once you get your foundation in place and maintain it, you will see your wealth start to increase.

Practical Life Advice to Improve Success

Let us review some good common sense moves that will increase your chance of obtaining your goal of wealth building over a lifetime.

Choose a Spouse with Compatible Financial Goals

Finding and sticking with the right life partner, especially in the financial sense, can make or break your chances of becoming wealthy. In fact, according to the research of author and academic Dr. Thomas J. Stanley, self-made millionaires are far more likely than the general population to be and stay married to the same spouse for life.

It matters that you and your life partner both work towards the same financial agenda. If you seek early retirement, they help bring in extra income, or clip coupons to save more money and take advantage of compounding interest. If your priorities involve a debt-free lifestyle, they support this without secretly shopping behind your back.

Even "Good Debt" Isn't Really Good

With few exceptions, debt can serve as a form of bondage to enslave the borrower, often for years. Visualize your life with the freedom of not owing money on anything. Resist the urge to "keep up with the Joneses" and charge up credit cards for things like expensive clothes and lavish vacations. Make paying off your existing debt a priority. Some financial advisors say that borrowing to finance important items such as a home or education is "good debt," but people tend to choose much more expensive schools and houses when they pay for them with borrowed funds.

This overreaching can keep you in debt for years and cost you thousands of dollars in interest that could have funded your retirement goals. Many high-quality yet bargain-priced schools exist, and buying a home beneath your means allows for extra cash to pay off your mortgage early and load that money into savings and retirement investments.

Get Clear on Your Relationship with Money

This rule is less obvious, but if you don't like where your parents were financially at your age, make different, conscious choices for yourself and your family. During your upbringing, the way in which your parents managed their money has likely influenced your financial management today.

Money is nothing more than a piece of paper with the image of a famous person on it. But, when you understand what it represents to you, you gain insight into your spending, saving, and earning habits. If you have always felt that you don't deserve to earn a higher salary, live without debt, or have as much money as "other people," these beliefs can cause you to make poor financial choices that will hold you back.

Get in touch with your true thoughts and break through them so you can start building more wealth.

Take Advantage of Retirement Plans

Max out your contributions to retirement accounts each year. Especially if you are young, you have the distinct advantage of time, meaning additional years of compounding interest growth. If you have a 401(k) plan through your employer—especially if they match your contributions—pay into it to take advantage of that match.

You could also, on top of that, fund a Roth IRA with annual contributions. Avoid a common mistake: Do not borrow money out of your retirement accounts. You won't be able to contribute more funds until you pay back the loan. You might find it harder to make contributions in future years, plus you'll have missed out on accumulating interest on the borrowed funds. Find alternate ways to cover unexpected medical bills, college expenses, or improvements to your home.

Live Below Your Means and Increase Your Living Standard Slowly

Get comfortable saying "no" to items you cannot afford to pay for with cash. Overspending and getting into debt dramatically impact the funds you'll have available each month to fund your retirement.

Buy a home that costs no more than 25% of your monthly net pay and get a 15-year mortgage at a fixed rate. As you earn more, start making additional payments on your mortgage so that you can pay it off sooner and contribute that money to retirement savings. This way, you'll set yourself up for a well-funded retirement with no mortgage payments.

Fund Your Retirement Before the Kids' College Funds

This may not sit well with a lot of parents, but there's no guarantee your kids will want to attend college. However, there's a high degree of probability that you will retire, assuming you live long enough. If you can't afford to do both, prioritize retirement savings over saving for college.

Draw Social Security as Late as Possible

Instead of retiring and taking social security payments as soon as possible at 62, delay your social security claim. As of February 2018, if you were born before 1955 and wait until the full retirement age of 66, you'll receive 100% of your social security benefit.

If you delay retirement until age 70, you'll receive a bonus, which puts your benefit at 132% of the amount you'd receive each month if you had retired at 66. Don't wait on applying for Medicare though; you'll need to apply by age 65 to avoid possible increased costs.

Now that I have given you a detailed blue print for obtaining wealth on a daily basis with a step--by-step approach, we will conclude the book with the chapter which introduces you to the "85/15 Financial Fitness Program" designed to help you achieve these goals. After you read the last chapter, you should be motivated enough to get on the road to financial success step by step regardless of your current income level.

CHAPTER 10

The 85/15 Financial Fitness Program

Before I introduce you to the 85/15 Financial Fitness Program, let me take a minute to share my personal testimony regarding my decision to enroll as a business major in college. I am so happy and content that I went to school to become an accountant. It is one of the best decisions that I made in my lifetime. You see, everyone should be an accountant to one degree or another. Since we all have to handle money on a daily basis, we should endeavor to understand financial terms and concepts to the best of our ability. We will further discuss this issue in the 85/15 Financial Fitness Program when we talk about the subject of financial literacy. In addition, the field is wide and expanding. As an accountant, I enjoyed a broad spectrum of jobs and duties in the field of accounting and business. It gave me the experience I needed to hustle in my own business, making even more money on the side. But the best part of being an accountant, budget manager, financial analyst, tax preparer, and Vice President of Finance was that it equipped me with the necessary experience needed to manage my own personal finances and investments at a level greater than the average person! I recommend that every individual take the time to learn effective personal financial management and share these concepts with their children at a very young age.

85/15 Financial Fitness Program ©1996

I developed the 85/15 Financial Fitness Program quite a few years ago to teach individuals and families how to effectively live on a level less than 100% of their after-tax take-home income. The primary focus is on budgeting, saving, and investing in an effort to reach future financial goals and wealth building. The 85/15 Financial Fitness Program incorporates two basic principles that are extremely necessary for financial success and wealth building: *financial literacy* and *financial discipline*.

Financial Literacy

Financial literacy is the ability to use knowledge and skills to manage one's financial resources effectively for a lifetime of financial security. Financial literacy is not the same for everyone; it is subject to variables such as age, family, lifestyle, culture, and place of residence.

The definition of financial literacy encompasses more than just personal finances. To be financially literate, an individual needs to be fluent in personal finances, global economics, entrepreneurship, and investing. Personal finance has moved beyond merely balancing your checkbook and saving for a rainy day. Most banking and financial transactions happen online in real time, and they can involve and intersect with several institutions and individuals in a matter of seconds. It is necessary to understand how to navigate personal finance technology at an early age.

It is simply not enough for an individual to work hard and earn money. You need to make the money that you earn work hard for you. Investing is the greatest source of accumulating and maintaining wealth. There is a myriad of ways to invest, allowing even the hard-working individual to grow their finances and build wealth.

Public education does not cover financial literacy. While it is necessary for students to be financially literate in order to be prepared for college and careers, schools struggle to achieve that goal. What skills to include, how to make the curriculum apply to all students, and how to instruct students that financial literacy directly impacts their lives are all unanswered questions for most schools.

A 2016 study estimated that nearly two-thirds of Americans couldn't pass a basic financial literacy test. Worse, the percentage of those who can pass the test has fallen consistently since the financial crisis to 37% last year (2015), from 42% in 2009.

Here is a basic test of your financial literacy you can take right now! "If you take out a $1,000 loan that has a 20% interest rate, how much will you owe in interest at the end of one year?" The answer is $200, but if you got that wrong, you're not alone. Nearly two-thirds of Americans can't calculate interest payments correctly. About a third said they didn't even know the first step in calculating interest payments. Bonds presented one of the biggest problems for respondents of the survey. Just 28% knew what happens to bond prices when interest rates fall (they rise). And less than half of all Americans appear to be able to answer basic questions about financial risk.

These findings come from the National Capability Study by the FINRA Foundation, which surveyed 27,564 Americans from June through October of 2015. FINRA is a private self-regulatory organization that oversees member brokers and securities traders.

One of the silver linings of the recent financial crisis was that it was supposed to have taught many Americans a painful lesson about the dangers of debt. Apparently, the message didn't get across. This study also showed that even eight years after the financial crisis, significant segments of the population, including African Americans, Latinos, women, Millennials, and people lacking a high school education are still worse off than before the recession. Thirty-nine percent of African Americans and 34% of Latinos have used such high-cost forms of borrowing as pawn shops and pay day loans, compared with 21% of Whites and 21% of Asians. And unlike their predecessors, 29% of Millennials, who are 18 to 34, said they had been late making mortgage payments versus 16% of those aged 35 to 54. And 45% of all respondents with no college education said if they had an emergency requiring them to pull together $2,000 within a month, they wouldn't be able to do so. The struggle is real!

"This research underscores the critical need for innovative strategies to equip consumers with the tools and education required to effectively manage their financial lives," said FINRA Foundation Chairman Richard Ketchum in a press release.

If you are not fortunate to be raised in a household where financial literacy is taught and promoted, you can go literally a lifetime without understanding basic financial concepts. There are only a few places where you can go to get a better understanding of financial concepts. So, if you don't learn these important concepts at school or in the home, what can you do? The 85/15 Financial Fitness Program is designed to help Americans of all ages learn effective financial management and literacy. You are never too young or old to get started.

When we talk about the subject of financial literacy, the very first concept you must understand and master is the value of one dollar in today's society, especially in a global marketplace. Until you finally wake up and realize your earning potential is based on the value of one dollar, you will never be prepared for financial success and wealth building in today's climate. Many ethnic groups and foreigners come to America with nothing and get rich over time because they understand and value one dollar. Understanding the value of one dollar simply means that you are not willing to spend more on the purchase of goods and services than you have to, and especially not more than they are worth.

Instead of feeling sorry for yourself and your financial condition, become more proactive with your efforts to climb out of your current situation. Make every dollar count. Be aware of your financial environment and the opportunities all around you. Become a comparison shopper. Learn how to wait on opportunities to purchase goods and services when they are on sale or discount.

Another thing you want to do on your road financial literacy is to change the types of books you read to include such titles as *Forbes* and *Business Week*, just to name a few. Educating yourself on current business practices and financial global markets is a continuous journey. We live in an economic climate that is changing on a daily basis. In addition, there are literally millions of articles on the subject of personal financial management on the Internet. With today's search engines and technological advances, googling these articles and blogs is very simple.

Teach Your Children the Value of a Dollar

If we are ever going to become serious about bringing a change in the way we budget, save, and invest, it must start with teaching your children the value of a dollar.

When parents are trying to save and invest money, they should make it a goal to include the whole family in the effort. This involves teaching their kids how important it is to save and invest. As simple as it may sound, this task is often very challenging. Here are two important tips that you can use in your efforts to get your children off to a good financial start and promote financial literacy.

1. Practice what you preach

If you ever spent time with kids, you know that they pay more attention to what you do than what you say. They imitate the actions of the adults around them, especially their parents. If your kids see you saving and investing money, chances are that they will want to do the same. Teach your kids to budget, save, and invest for their future. Help them to understand that sometimes you have to wait to make purchases of goods and services. Help them to learn at an early age that patience is a virtue!

2.   Match your child's contributions

Just as many companies have programs in which they match retirement contributions, you can give your kids the same kind of incentive and bonus for saving. As he or she saves, match them penny for penny or dollar for dollar. This will teach them the art of saving and investing at an early age and these habits will most likely follow them throughout their lifetime.

Financial Discipline

Financial discipline refers to how well you are able to conform your spending and saving to the plans that you have set to achieve your monetary goals. Make a written plan of action! If you don't have a financial plan in place, it's really hard to be disciplined about how you spend your money because you haven't created any guidelines for yourself to follow.

In my line of business as a personal financial consultant, I get asked a range of financial questions from "How do I save more money?" to "How do I tackle huge amounts of debt?" to "How do I stop living from paycheck to paycheck?" At the root of all these challenges is financial discipline. I often remind my clients that If you continue to spend 100% or more of your after-tax take-home income, known as *net* income, you will never be worth more tomorrow than you are today." You will never grow financial wealth or obtain the American dream. Even worse, you will never be able to leave an inheritance to your children, perpetuating the cycle of starting from zero from generation to generation.

Most people in America live with the misconception that a lack of money is the reason why they can't get ahead financially. Many of the clients that I meet with tell me that they don't make enough, but the real deal is if you have a lack of financial discipline, you will always struggle with money problems whether you make $10,000 a year or $10 million a year.

One of my common phrases that I often say to my clients is, "It's not how much you make, but it's what you do with it that will determine your future financial condition!"

Discipline in general is not one of those sexy words or concepts that most of us embrace or enjoy talking about. In our current culture, we're encouraged to "have it all now!" Everyone is on monthly payments in an effort to "keep up with the Joneses" as we say. But spending 100% of your net income or even more through the use of credit card debt will leave you stressed, depressed, and often enslaved to your debt and lifestyle.

The good news is anyone can develop financial discipline (yes, that includes you!). When we talk about financial discipline, we are talking about *behavior modification*. You have to change your behavior and the way you do things. Most psychologist and doctors would tell you that behavior modification usually takes place over a period of time and requires a constant stimulus. If you have ever lost weight or gotten yourself in physical shape, you understand that change can be slow and is often a step-by-step journey that requires long-term commitment.

If you are really serious about changing your financial condition, you need to get mad. You need to get so mad at your situation that you have to do something about it, no matter what stands in your way. Getting your emotions involved helps to keep you engaged in the process. If you have a laid-back attitude towards making a change, you probably won't change. As you get older, you will better understand the pain and disappointment of not disciplining yourself when you were younger, especially as you approach the age of retirement. Unfortunately, it will be too late to realize that the pain of spending 100% or more of your income is much greater than the temporary satisfaction that you received from the purchasing of goods and services that you though would bring you joy and happiness.

Much has been written about the "sandwich generation": middle-aged Americans who are caught between their financial obligations to elderly parents who are living longer, and their children, while also trying to prepare for their own retirement years.

Yet millions of Americans face an even bigger bind: More than one-third of all working-age adults haven't managed to save money toward retirement, according to a survey by Bankrate.com. The personal finance site found that 26% of people age 50-to-54-years-old and 14% of those aged 65 and older have no savings at all.

If you are serious about changing your financial habits and becoming more financially disciplined, then you need to get "financially naked!" Getting financially naked simply means that you have to stop financing your current lifestyle with credit card debt. You are living at a lever greater than 100% of your net income. One of the biggest reasons why many people can't change their financial situation is because they are addicted to using credit cards and cannot or do not pay off the outstanding balance at the end of each month. Using credit cards without paying off the outstanding balance each month is like eating ice cream each night before bed and wondering why you're not losing weight. The struggle is real regardless of how much you earn if you don't have financial discipline.

Let us take a close look at the athletic arena and what happens to many sports celebrities who earn millions during their career.

Professional athletes are paid millions of dollars because they are the best people on the planet at what they do and what they do just happens to generate billions of dollars in revenue every year. However, with fame and money comes a lot of pressure to provide for your family, close and extended, friends real and fake, and significant others. Add to that equation the cadre of agents, managers, and financial advisors who see the athletes as meal tickets, and it becomes easier to see how many end up filing for bankruptcy once their playing days are over.

A 2009 Sports Illustrated study found that 78% of NFL players either file for bankruptcy or struggle financially once they retire. About 60% of NBA players face similar financial struggles five years after they retire.

Planning for retirement is key, and part of that goes to saving and budgeting for your golden years. It is a good policy to stay on top of your own investments to protect yourself and your earnings. There are countless incidences of athletes being defrauded by financial advisors that they trusted after the funds they invested were stolen, embezzled, or mismanaged. Investment management company Vanguard says players should be meeting basic living expenses, establishing reserve funds, and leaving a legacy. Discretionary spending, like fancy clothes and a car for mom, should be limited. Listed below are just five Athletes who filed bankruptcy after their career days were over.

1. Mike Tyson is a former professional boxer who competed from 1995 to 2005. He reigned as the undisputed world heavyweight champion and holds the record as the youngest boxer to win a heavy weight title at 20 years old. Mike Tyson's career earnings were estimated at over $400 million.

2. Allen Iverson, nicknamed "The Answer," is a former professional basketball player. He played for 14 seasons in the NBA as both the shooting guard and point guard. Iverson was an 11-time NBA All-Star, won the All-Star game MVP award in 2001 and 2005, and the All-Star NBA Most Valuable Player in 2001. He was inducted into the National Memorial Basketball Hall of Fame in 2016. Allen Iverson's career earnings were estimated at $150 million.

3. Boris Becker is a former No. 1 professional world tennis player. He won the first of his six major singles titles at age 17. He also won five year-end championships, 13 Masters Series titles, and an Olympic gold medal in doubles. Boris Becker's career earnings were estimated at $126 million.

4. Antoine Walker is a former professional basketball player. He was the sixth overall pick in the 1996 NBA Draft out of the University of Kentucky and played in the NBA from 1996 to 2008. Walker played for the Celtics, Mavericks, Hawks, Heat, Timberwolves, the BSN's Mets, and the NBA D-league's Stampede before retiring from basketball in 2012. Antoine Walker's career earnings were estimated at $108 million.

5. John Daly is an American professional golfer on the PGA Tour. Daly is known primarily for his driving distance off the tee, his non-country club appearance and attitude, his exceptionally long backswing, the inconsistency of his play, and his rough-and-tumble personal life. John Daly's career earnings were estimated at $57 million.

The list of athletes, entertainers, singers, rappers and Hollywood actors and actresses who have gone bankrupt is endless! Some even have served time in jail for unpaid taxes and tax evasion. So, you can see that how much you earn has nothing to do with the level of financial discipline needed to successfully manage your financial success.

Once again, as long as you spend 100% or more of your net income, you will never be worth more tomorrow than you are today. It doesn't matter if you earn $10,000 a year or $400 million a year. There is no end to spending money. Until you understand the art of "paying yourself first" before you begin spending, you will never enjoy financial success. The road to financial success starts with financial discipline and financial literacy.

The million-dollar question is why does the 85/15 Financial Fitness Program make sense? What is it about 85% that is so special and unique? The answer to that question is that it allows you to set a goal that is realistic and attainable. Although practically anyone can benefit from this program, it is geared towards those individuals who are currently living at a level of 100% or more of their net income. The two factors that make it a great program is the percentage of income devoted to current lifestyle and the fact that it's percentage based.

Most would agree that 85% of anything is very good. This program does not require an unrealistic approach to money management. As stated earlier, most individuals who work from week to week and paycheck to paycheck need some sort of immediate gratification or reward system for their hard work. Establishing a budget that requires a great commitment and change in spending habits usually fails in the long run. Instead, these goals are very realistic and obtainable by most individuals without sacrificing their current lifestyle. It is my belief through much research and experience that most individuals can carve out 15% of their current expense without a major change in the current lifestyle that they have been accustom too. Asking individuals to make great sacrifices and reductions in spending usually result in an abandonment of the budget over time because of frustration. By simply applying more thought and time in the budget process, most individuals can reduce their overall expense by 15% or more over a short period of time.

Let us remember that 85% is the end goal and not the beginning. Of course, those individuals who are currently spending more than 100% of their income a month through credit card purchases will need a longer period of time to reach the goal of 85%. Just like losing weight or getting in shape, this is a daily step-by-step process, but if you remain committed and faithful to your financial goals you can get there no matter how long it takes.

The great thing about percentage-based budgeting is that it is relative regardless of income level. Whether you bring home $10,000 a year or $10 million, 85% is still 85% across the board. The key is to "stay in your lane" regardless of how much you earn. Later in this chapter we will discuss "the power of the 15%" and how you can save and invest over time regardless of your income level.

There are three keys in this program that help to unlock the door to financial success:

Key #1 - A budget which is a written well-thought-out plan of action
Key #2 - Monthly compliance check. You are required to attend a monthly meeting where we review your financial progress
Key #3 - Monthly motivational seminars and workshops

Keys #1 and #2 help to open the door to financial discipline while key #3 opens the door to financial literacy.

Key #1: Budget

We help you to establish a household budget if you do not have one already. If you have a budget already then you will only need to modify your model to incorporate our spending levels. In our budget model, individuals learn how to effectively budget to save and invest by "paying themselves first" before they start spending. We will teach you how to track your expenses and learn the areas where you are wasting the most money. Our program helps you to establish a spending threshold less than 100% of your net income. For those of you who have no clue as where to begin the process, this is an excellent program. If you are currently saving more than 15% of your income, then this program may not be for you. However, you can still benefit from the other components of the program.

According to economist Dennis Jacobe, a 2013 Gallup poll indicated that roughly one in three Americans prepare a detailed household budget that includes financial planning and investment goals. Those with at least some college education, conservatives, Republicans, Independents, and those making $75,000 a year or more are slightly more likely to prepare a detailed household budget than are their counterparts.

These results are from Gallup's annual Economy and Personal Finance survey, conducted in April 2013. Gallup asked Americans about several types of financial management tools to gauge how they track their finances.

Key #2: Compliance

The subject of compliance deals with accountability. Compliance promotes accountability! It is a term that many accountants like myself and other business-minded individuals are very familiar with through our line of work. Whether it's an internal auditor, external auditor, or review board, those of us in the field of business understand the importance of periodic review to ensure compliance not only to laws and regulations, but also to make sure that a business is on track with its mission statement and company goals. The first step in the process is the creation of budget as previously discussed. The next step is a usually monthly review of financial transactions relating to income and expenses. As a financial analyst, I gained much experience in preparing financial statements that involved budget to actual comparisons to determine budget short-falls and overages. Our program does not try to turn you into an accountant, but to equip you with the tools that you need to manage your personal finances.

As an accountant and Vice President of Finance, I learned through the years the importance of compliance. Most corporations, both profit and non-profit, understand that at year end they will undergo an annual audit and review of their financial records to assure investors and other third-party individuals with a vested interest in the organization that the accounting records have been maintained according to "general accepted accounting principles" (GAAP). Most companies want to receive a good review at the end of the fiscal year by the audit firm that they engaged, better known in the business arena as an unqualified opinion. An unqualified opinion simply states that the financial statements in review are free from material mistakes and are a "fair representation of the activities" that took place during the period under review. It does not say that the financial records are perfect.

From this process I learned quickly that when you know that you will be reviewed periodically to analyze your financial record keeping and financial progress, it will cause you to be more conscious of your actions. Applying this same theory to the 85/15 Financial Fitness Program means that the element of financial review on a periodic basis will further your motivation to stay focused on your budget and financial goals that you have set.

In our program, we recommend that you attend a compliance meeting to review your financial progress on a monthly basis. A monthly review of your budget and financial goals will better help us to determine where you need to focus your efforts. We will be able to quickly identify the areas where you have exceeded budget and maybe need to make modifications to your budget and goals. Without the element of monthly compliance, the temptation to cheat yourself is greater. If no one is watching over you, then you may be inclined to revert back to your old habits.

Key #3: Financial Seminars and Workshops

The purpose of our financial seminars and workshops is to help you to maintain motivation. As most of you know, the level of motivation that individuals experience usually changes over time. The longer an individual goes without some sort of stimulus, the more likely the motivational level will dissipate. Unless motivational levels are rekindled by repeated stimuli, most individuals will lose interest and fall back into their old habits. In other words, we are talking about behavior modification. When you read my book, you will probably be very motivated to make a change in the way you manage your personal finance, but over time you will lose that motivation. By placing you in a room once a month with other individuals who share your passion for financial success and change, you will be able to rekindle any motivation that you may have lost during the month.

The second purpose of our seminars and workshops is to promote financial literacy. Unless you have gone to a college or university to study business, you most likely have never been exposed to many financial terms and practices. Since personal financial management is not taught in schools in America, most individuals have never had the opportunity to be exposed to current business practices. Let us take a lesson from the 78% of NFL athletes who went broke roughly five years after retirement after making millions of dollars. Having a financial advisor is good but understanding financial concepts for yourself is even better. Ultimately, it's your responsibility to make sure that your financial success is maintained throughout the remainder of your life and even beyond as an inheritance to your children.

So, you can see that the need for this kind of financial fitness program is overwhelming. Roughly two-thirds of our current population go day to day without a budget or written plan of financial goals. Now let us take a closer look at a secret key that makes this program a jewel.

The 85% of household budget that we recommend you live on is further divided between *essential* and *non-essential* expenses. We recommend that you budget 65% of your income for essential expenses relating to the operation of your household. In addition, we recommend that you budget 20% of your income for non-essential expenses, better known as the "joy and entertainment budget."

Your 65% Essential Household Budget

In our budget model, we suggest that you keep your essential or household expenses to a level of 65%. Please keep in mind that this target is the endgame plan and not the beginning. It is our belief that anyone can become financially fit over time if they apply themselves to our program. If you are currently spending more than 100% of your income, then it only means that it may take you a little longer than others to get to the target goal. But rest assured, if you stay committed you will get there eventually.

Your 20% Joy and Entertainment Budget

As we stated earlier, most successful household budgets have an element of immediate gratification or joy. Most individuals who work from week to week and paycheck to paycheck need some sort of immediate reward for their efforts. Whether it's going out to a movie, sports event, concert, getting your nails done, or going out to dinner, we all have non-essential spending habits. The problem is that without a budget that restricts these types of expenses to a specific amount, in many instances, spending gets out of hand. As we said earlier, many individuals are caught up in impulse spending on goods and services that don't provide the level of satisfaction that was expected. How many times have you made a purchase of a goods or services that didn't bring you the level of satisfaction that you expected?

We also discussed the theory of the law of diminishing return, which is the principle that the more frequently you engage in an activity, the less joy you receive from that activity. The example that we gave earlier relates to going out to dinner. If you go out to dinner three times in one week, there is less joy and satisfaction in the third dinner than the first dinner. If you are going out to dinner three times a week throughout the month, then if you cut back to once a week or twice a month you will enjoy each dinner more. This theory is not an absolute science and there are exceptions to the rule, but in general it applies to most activities. In addition, we discussed the theory of the joy of anticipation. There is a certain residual benefit in anticipating an activity. If you plan in advance to go to dinner once a week, the mere fact that you anticipate this event will create a certain level of satisfaction. It's like a benchmark to help you sustain yourself until you get to the next level.

The goal of this budget is to assist you with your efforts to eliminate financial waste. By simply applying more thought into how you spend your hard-earned income, will help you to avoid unnecessary expenses that eat up your potential savings. If you are currently spending at a level equal to 100% of your net income, then this program is for you. We believe that we can help you to cut around 15% of your current expense without a major change in lifestyle. Not asking you to make a major change in lifestyle is a key benefit of our program.

So, in summary, the 65% budget of essential spending and the 20% of non-essential spending make up the total 85% budget for current living expenses.

Now that we have shared with you the 85% living expense budget, it's time to share with you the "power of the 15%."

Your 15% Long-term Savings and Investments

The main goal of this program is to get more Americans to save and invest at least 15% of their net. As previously stated, wealth building for most Americans is a step-by-step process. Once you stop spending 100% or more of your net income, you will be in a position to start saving and investing in your future.

Step one in this process is to establish an emergency reserve fund for rainy days. You can be sure that eventually an unexpected expense will take place in your life. What happens if you lose your job? Can you still pay your bills and survive until you find new employment? The majority of Americans can't survive more than 30 days without their current income. In our program, we help you to establish an emergency reserve fund which is equal to six months of your current budget.

As you begin to establish your emergency reserve fund, one thing that you may consider (if you don't already have one), is a pre-paid credit card. You can kill two birds with one stone by securing a pre-paid credit card. A pre-paid credit card, better known as a secured credit card, requires you to pre-pay an amount equal to your available credit limit. By doing this, you can increase your credit score in the process. Once you establish a good repayment history most card holders can increase their credit limit and, in some cases, move from a secured credit card to an unsecured credit card as your credit score improves. The object is to pay the total outstanding balance off at the end of the period, thereby avoiding monthly interest and fees relating to card usage.

Your 5% Emergency Reserve Fund

In our program, we encourage you to set aside 5% (or one-third of the 15%) into an emergency reserve fund. Each month, when you first get started, you will need to set aside 5% until your emergency reserve fund reaches a level which is equal to six months of your current budget. After you reach this level, the entire 15% will go towards long-term savings and investments. If an emergency arrives and you need to take money from the emergency fund, you simply go back to setting aside 5% until the reserve fund is replenished back to a level equal to six months of your expenses.

Your 10% Long-term Savings and Investments

While in the process of establishing your emergency reserve fund, you will save 10% of your income for long-term savings and investments. When your emergency reserve fund reaches a level equal to six months of your expenses you will then begin to save the entire 15% in long-term savings and investments. The younger you are when you start this program, the better off you will be. You are never too young to begin our program. Even children who receive a weekly allowance or earn money from chores or part time work can start our program. You are never too old to start our program, either. Just because you didn't start to save and invest at an early age doesn't mean you have to give up on your dreams.

As previously stated, "It's not how much you earn, but what you do with it!" Let us discover together the "power of the 15%" and its ability to open the door to financial success and wealth building. Even though I am not a registered investment broker or agent, as a financial professional with much experience in the field, I will try to help you to better understand the many opportunities that exist for potential investors and entrepreneurs of all ages.

Most people never get involved with saving and investing because they don't know where to begin. Let us hold your hand as we walk you down the path of saving and investing step by step. This is not an exact science and the possibilities are limitless, but we will try to give you an idea and a better understanding of how to get in the game and get started on the road to financial success.

The Road to Savings and Investing

As we get on the road to long-term savings and investing, we must consider two factors: age and risk tolerance. The younger you are, usually the greater the risk tolerance. Most investment advisors recommend a lower risk tolerance for older investors. The age factor becomes very important because when you are younger, you have more time to rebound from potential losses on investments. In addition, most investment vehicles tend to yield higher returns over a long period of time. If you invest in a vehicle that has a high rate of return, it may produce a loss in the short run but a gain over a longer period of time. Unfortunately, as you age, you often don't have the opportunity to let your investments sit while waiting for a return on investment. If you need to access these funds, you will most likely have to take a loss on your investments.

We will try to share with you some investment vehicles that have little or no risk, as well as more riskier investments that in many cases offer a greater return on investments. In general, the higher the risk on investment, the higher the return. We recommend that you never leave your hard-earned money in the hands of an investment broker or advisor without having at least a basic understanding of investment strategies. Ultimately, the "buck stops with you," and it is your responsibility to ensure that you are investing according to your desires and abilities. Let us take a lesson from the many athletes and entertainers that have lost their entire fortunes by simply placing the responsibility of money management and investing in the hands of a trusted broker or investment advisor.

Savings Accounts

As we get on the road to long-term savings and investments, let's start with one of the most basic and safe investment vehicles: a savings account.

As I took a quick look at the current opportunities to establish a savings account, I discovered that you can open a savings account with no fees and earn an interest rate of between 2.0% and 2.5% on monies deposited. These accounts usually offer a fixed rate of interest on your balance and are insured by the FDIC (up to $250,000 in deposits). Now, you may not get rich from this form of investment, but it's a start on the path of financial success.

A recent survey conducted by Google on its finance website GoBankingRates.com discovered that approximately 62% of Americans have less than $1,000 in their savings accounts and 21% don't even have a savings account. "It's worrisome that such a large percentage of Americans have so little set aside in a savings account," says Cameron

Huddleston, a personal finance analyst for the site. "They likely don't have cash reserves to cover an emergency and will have to rely on credit, friends and family, or even their retirement accounts to cover unexpected expenses."

A savings account is a great place to get started if you don't have much money to set aside. After research, I discovered that you can open a savings account online with a minimum deposit of between $1 and $25, so there is no excuse to not get started on the right road. Maybe it's time that you take the first step!

Savings Bonds

Investing in bonds for income can result in predictable returns as compared to when you invest in the stock market. Bonds fall under the category of fixed income investment instruments due to their guaranteed interest payments along with the principal payment at maturity.

One of the most important reasons to invest in bonds is that they play a key role in diversifying your portfolio. Bonds are significantly less volatile than stocks and can help control overall portfolio volatility. While bond returns exceed stock returns infrequently, they have exceeded stock returns during some periods of significant negative stock performance like 2001, 2002, and 2008, protecting the overall portfolio from a big loss. A wise and prudent investor knows when to move investments from one investment instrument to another based on business climate.

The million-dollar question is, "How much do I need to start investing in the bond market?" The minimum size of a bond depends on the type of bond, and these amounts vary from issuer to issuer. At the smaller end are US Treasury Securities, which can be purchased in $100 increments.

Penny Stocks

Buying penny stocks is one of the fastest ways to turn a relatively small amount of money into a relatively large amount of money, period.

If you invested just $1,000 in MNST (Monster Beverage Corp) when it was trading around $0.07 per share, you'd have earned well over $850,000 today. This represents the power of the penny stock at its best!

If you enjoy gambling and are willing to put your capital on the line, penny stocks provide ample opportunity to profit. If you want to save yourself time and money, consider joining the thousands of investors who subscribe to *Stock Advisor* to find new stocks every week that are statistically likely to increase in value.

Lending Clubs

Lending Club, located in San Francisco, California, operates a *peer-to-peer* lending company for personal loans. The company assesses the applicant's risk and lets investors lend directly to individuals or spread their money across a number of loans. Lending Club was founded in 2006.

The Cannabis Industry

One of the fastest growth industries is the marijuana business. One of the biggest producers of cannabis on the planet is Canopy Growth Corporation (TSX: Weed). Cannabis is now considered the largest crop in the US. It's bigger than corn, bigger than cotton, and bigger than wheat. The current cannabis market is valued at $142 billion.

Imagine putting $50,000 in Aphria Inc. (NYSE: APHA) in early 2016 and cashing out less than two years later. That would've put an extra $1.1

million into your pocket. You can start investing in the cannabis industry for as little as $1,000.

Crowdfunding

One of the best companies loaning money to start-ups and existing businesses is a company called NextSeed.

By using the latest crowdfunding laws and technology, NextSeed is creating new opportunities for businesses and everyday investors to grow together. Through NextSeed, small businesses have access to a source of debt financing that is all around them. Crowdfunding on NextSeed helps a business bring on investors from the community, who can become customers, raving fans, and loyal advocates of the business.

Anyone in the US, regardless of income or net worth, can now begin investing in restaurants, bars, fitness studios, and other local businesses. Investments start as low as $100, giving everyday people a real opportunity to start building a portfolio of loan investments.

NextSeed was the first SEC registered funding portal under the JOBS Act and closed the first ever Regulation Crowdfunding offering in July 2016.

Real Estate

One of the best opportunities to start investing in the real estate market with as little as $500, is a company called Fundrise. Fundrise has historically earned a return on investment of between 8.7% and 12.4%. Fundrise has invested $2.5 billion in real estate. By pursuing a private market, direct investment strategy, Fundrise portfolios earn higher annual current income than public income-focused investments like public bonds and public real estate.

ETF (Exchange Traded Fund)

An ETF, or Exchange Traded Fund, is in essence a combination of an index mutual fund and a stock fund. Whereas with mutual funds you can only trade at the end of the day, ETFs allow you to buy and sell whenever the market is open. This gives the investor more control over ETF holdings. The simplicity and low cost of ETFs make them a highly popular investment choice, even for the most conservative investor. You can start investing in ETFs with as little as $500. With over 700 ETFs on the market today, there's sure to be one that fits your investment style.

There are many opportunities to begin investing regardless of how much you have to get started. The object is not to get rich from investing but to become a savvy investor who understands the art of investing and maximizing income.

Let us give a final review of the five areas of personal financial management that may indicate that you are on the road to becoming financially fit!

1. A written budget: you must prepare a written budget that is well thought out and realistic
2. Long-term savings and investments at 15%: you should be setting aside at least 15% of your income for long-term savings and investments
3. A credit score of 680: you should have a credit score of 680 or better
4. Reserve fund: you should have an emergency reserve fund equal to 6 months of your budget
5. Financial literacy: you must understand basic financial terms and business practices

Although there are many ways to budget, save, and invest, the 86/15 financial fitness program is a great place to start for anyone who doesn't have a clue as to where to get started.

References

"Fraud is on the Rise and Small Businesses May Bear the Brunt of the Impact," by Shazir Mucklai. www.homeofscience.net. May 2020.

Psychology of Money, Dr James Gottfurcht. www.psychologyofmoney.com 2018

Power of 5 Senses, By Surinder Leen. https://www.powerof5senses.com/. January 2018.

"Top 10 Poorest Countries in The World 2019," Oasdom: The Business Oasis. https://www.oasdom.com/poorest-country-in-the-world/ May 28, 2019

"6 Ways to Instill a Positive Money Mindset," by Rebecca Jackson. https://www.mint.com/vip-content/6-ways-to-instill-a-positive-money-mindset. December 2014,

"How Do Black People Spend Their Money?" By Gary A. Johnson. *Black Men in America*. https://blackmeninamerica.com/updated-how-do-black-people-spend-their-money-3/. September 29, 2019.

"New Attitudes Towards Wealth," *US History Online Textbook.* US History.org. https://www.ushistory.org/us/36e.asp. 2020.

"Why Rich People Get Richer – The #1 Main Reason," by Derek with Life and My Finances. https://lifeandmyfinances.com/2020/04/why-rich-people-get-richer-the-1-main-reason/. April 17, 2020.

"The 3 Richest Americans Hold More Wealth Than Bottom 50% Of The Country, Study Finds," by Noah Kirsch. *Forbes.https://www.forbes.com/sites/noahkirsch/2017/11/09/the-3-richest-americans-hold-more-wealth-than-bottom-50-of-country-study-finds/#4f60cd13cf86.* November 9, 2017

"Racial Wealth Gap in the United States," by Kimberly Amadeo. *The Balance.* https://www.thebalance.com/racial-wealth-gap-in-united-states-4169678. April 27, 2020.

"22 Legit Ways to Get Rich People to Give You Money Online," by Amy Kennedy. *Work at Home Adventures.* https://wahadventures.com/get-rich-people-give-you-money/. April 20, 2020.

"10 Most Unethical Business Practices in Big Business," *Business Pundit.* https://www.businesspundit.com/10-most-unethical-business-practices/. November 14, 2013.

"The Racial Wealth Gap: Addressing America's Most Pressing Epidemic," by Brian Thompson. https://www.forbes.com/sites/brianthompson1/2018/02/18/the-racial-wealth-gap-addressing-americas-most-pressing-epidemic/#572e907e7a48. February 18, 2018.

"What is Money?" *Investopedia.* https://www.investopedia.com/insights/what-is-money/. June 26, 2019.

"7 Smart Ways to Invest $1,000," by Jeff Rose. *Forbes*. www.forbes.com/2019/how to invest 1,000. October 22, 2019.

"The Richest Countries in the World," by James Burton. *World Atlas*. https://www.worldatlas.com/articles/the-richest-countries-in-the-world.html. January 7, 2020.

"The World's Top 10 Economies by GDP," by Raphael Zeder. *Quicknomics*. https://quickonomics.com/the-worlds-top-10-economies-by-gdp/. June 7, 2019.

Mind Over Money: The Psychology of Money and How To Use It Better. By Claudia Hammond. Harper Collins: New York, NY. 2016.

"All about the dollar, it makes me want to holler, makes me want to scream, it's not about the color white, not about the color black, but all about the color green!" is a slogan often used by Jerome Kirkland on radio broadcasts.

All About the Dollar is an extraordinary look at money and the role it plays in everyday life. It is a thought-provoking look into the history of money, global economics, American wealth and spending habits, and finally, a program that provides a solution to changing those spending habits and starting on the road to wealth building.

This is a book for everyone who has thought that wealth building was an impossible goal, especially for those who are living on low or fixed income. You are never too young or old to get on the road to financial literacy and wealth building. Budgeting, saving, and investing is a process that requires discipline and understanding.

Jerome Kirkland is a native of Buffalo, New York, and a benefactor of the desegregation movement of the late 1960s and early 1970s when inner city black children were bused out to predominately white schools. He was the only negro student in his first-grade class. By the end of the year, he was an honor student. This was the beginning of a great academic experience that would last a lifetime. In addition, it was this experience that caused him to embrace people of all races, colors, creeds, and religious persuasions.

Jerome is a graduate of Temple University School of Business with a BBA in Accounting and more than 30 years in the business and accounting industry, serving for-profit and nonprofit corporations, businesses, and individuals. He brings to the table a wealth of knowledge and insight regarding income and wealth-building as well as managing business and personal expenses. He is a budget guru. He has hosted a financial broadcast on the Philadelphia- based radio station WURD 900 and has appeared on the radio station Power 99. He has been a licensed mortgage broker and a professional tax consultant. He currently owns a financial consulting business, Kirkland Financial Group, headquartered in Philadelphia Pennsylvania. It caters to small businesses and individuals who want to better their financial situation. He is the author and creator of the "85/15 Financial Fitness Program" which provides the three keys to unlocking the door to successful financial management. He is also the author and creator of the "1065 Business Partnership Program" which provides financial support, insight, and management to those who own a struggling business or want to start a new business venture.

CPSIA information can be obtained
at www.ICGtesting.com
Printed in the USA
BVHW031624130720
583630BV00001B/86

9 781977 228598